Favourite
Dishes
of
India

KAUSHI BHATIA

ABOUT THE AUTHOR

KAUSHI N. BHATIA is a familiar name in the field of Indian and Chinese cookery. Her recipes and articles on cuisine have been published in many leading newspapers and magazines.

She has often held cooking demonstrations and been invited to judge cookery contests. She is the author of three other popular cookbooks *Indian Cookbook*, *Vegetarian Chinese Cookbook and Dollops Ice Creams and Desserts*.

All her books are popular and much appreciated for their simple and practical aproach. Her recipes can be easily prepared by beginners as well as experienced cooks.

Zaika is an imprint of
BUSINESS PUBLICATIONS INC
A Quartette Group Company

ISBN 81-86982-09-4
© Kaushi Bhatia, 1997
Cover design and illustrations by
    Kini Kaul, Minds Eye, Mumbai

Published by

Zaika

229/A Second Floor
Krantiveer Rajguru Marg
Girgaon   Mumbai 400 004

—— For ——

Naveen, my husband,
who inspired me and
occupied a distinctive place
on my panel of tasters.

CONTENTS

Gujarati

Hyderabadi

Kashmiri

Vegetrain

Rajasthani

Vegetarian

Sindhi

Non-Vegetarian

Vegetarian

South Indian

Non-Vegetarian

Vegetarian

 Main Dish | Side Dish | Snack | Dessert | Breakfast

INTRODUCTION

*G*one are the days when people stuck to their traditional food only. Now there is an enthusiastic trend to imbibe delicacies from different parts of India as well as from abroad. After an in–depth study and many interviews, I have made a selection of the best known and most popular Indian dishes. There are few cuisines in the world that can compete with the Indian in sheer variety of taste and presentation.

This book comprises of vegetarian and non-vegetarian recipes, keeping in mind the specialities of each community and including dishes for festive occasions. The special features of every dish have been highlighted in the form of a short introduction to each recipe. Helpful hints have been included wherever necessary so that there is absolutely no room for error.

While choosing the dishes, various aspects have been considered, such as the availability of ingredients, cost, time and method of cooking, taste, presentation and above all, nutrition.

There is a vast assortment of dishes to choose from, which can fit into menus for breakfast, brunch, lunch, an evening snack or dinner.

The methods suggested are simple, straightforward and least time consuming. Most of the dishes are economical, barring a few elaborate dishes, which are suitable for special occasions. The category into which every dish falls is also stated together with its main accompaniments.

All measures are in cups and spoons. There are dishes that need no oil (sure to delight the weight conscious) and dishes that require no cooking (for those in a hurry).

It is rightly said that variety is the spice of life.

Bengali

Bhappa Chingri
Steamed Prawns

Mustard oil is traditionally used in most Bengali dishes. However, any other oil may be used. Steaming not only makes this dish low-fat and aromatic but also preserves valuable nutrients, besides being a simple and time-saving method. The main accompaniment to this dish is rice or chappatis.

INGREDIENTS

2 cups shelled and deveined prawns
1 tsp turmeric powder
1 tsp chilli powder
½ cup grated coconut
1 tbsp coriander leaves
1 tbsp mustard oil
4 green chillies (slit through the centre,
seeds removed & base kept intact)
Salt to taste

To Grind
1 ½ tbsp mustard seeds
4 green chillies
A little water

MEHTOD

Wash the prawns well. Set aside.

Combine the mustard-green chilli paste, turmeric powder, chilli powder, coconut, coriander leaves and salt. Add the prawns to this mixture. Mix well so that the prawns are coated with this mixture. Place the masala coated prawns in a small container. Spread the oil all over the prawns. Top with the slit green chillies. Cover the container with a tight-fitting lid.

Pour about 2 cups water into a pressure cooker. Put the grid in it. Place the container with the prawns on the gird. Pressure cook till done i.e. after one whistle, switch off the gas. When the pressure cooker is opened, remove the container with the prawns, open it and serve the prawns hot with rice or chappatis.

SERVES : 4-6

Bhate Ilish

Rice with Hilsa Fish

A tiffin box containing spicy raw fish pieces is placed with rice, to cook. This dish is considered a delicacy.

INGREDIENTS

12 long thin pieces cut from the under belly of the Hilsa fish (as this part has fewer bones)

½ tsp turmeric powder
1 tbsp mustard seeds
2 green chillies
1 tbsp mustard oil
Salt to taste
} Grind to a paste using a little water

For The Rice
2 cups uncooked rice
4 cups water
No salt

MEHTOD

Clean and wash the fish pieces. Rub the turmeric powder and salt on the fish pieces and set aside for about 5 minutes. Then rub the mustard-green chilli paste on the fish pieces and put them in a tiffin box. Dribble the oil all round the fish pieces. Close the tiffin box. Set aside.

Pick and then wash the rice. Drain. Boil 4 cups of water and add the rice. Cook covered, on a low flame. When the rice is half-cooked, put the tiffin box right into the centre of the rice. Place the pan on a tawa. Cook covered on a low flame for about 7 minutes or until the rice is done, by which time the fish will also be cooked.

Serve the hot rice with the fish in the same tiffin box.

SERVES : 4-6

Chingri Bora
Fried Prawn Balls

*Delicately spiced, these unusual pakoras are indeed a
popular snack. While frying these pakoras, add a pinch of salt
to the hot oil to prevent the pakoras from sticking to the pan.
The main accompaniment to this dish is tomato ketchup.*

INGREDIENTS

2 ½ cups small-sized white prawns
(shelled & deveined)
1 cup gram flour
1 ½ cups chopped onion
4 green chillies chopped
½ cup chopped coriander leaves
Oil for frying
Salt to taste

To Rub On The Prawns
½ tsp turmeric powder
Salt to taste

METHOD

Wash the prawns. Rub with the mixture of turmeric powder and salt. Set aside for about 15 minutes. After 15 minutes, discard the water and remove the prawns carefully, without squeezing.

Combine the prawns, gram flour, onion, green chillies, coriander leaves and salt. Mix well, using 1 to 2 tablespoons of water (only if necessary) and prepare a smooth mixture.

Heat oil in a frying pan. Add a pinch of salt to the oil, as this will prevent the pakoras from sticking to the pan while frying. When the oil smokes, reduce flame to low. Make small lemon-sized balls from the mixture and deep fry a few balls at a time. Drain when golden brown in colour.

Serve hot with tomato ketchup as a snack, side dish or with cocktails.

SERVES : 4-6

Chingri Malai Kalai
Prawns in Coconut Milk

The coconut milk used in this dish gives it a distinctive look and taste which is unforgettable. The main accompaniment to this dish is rice or puris.

INGREDIENTS

8 medium–sized bagda prawns (king prawns)
3 tbsp oil
2 tbsp melted ghee
2 cloves
2 cardamoms
1" stick cinnamon
½ cup grated onion
2 green chillies (chopped)
1 tsp ground ginger
½ tsp chilli powder
½ tsp turmeric powder
1 tbsp sour curd
2 cups coconut milk
½ tsp sugar
Salt to taste

To Rub On The Prawns
½ tsp turmeric powder
Salt to taste

METHOD

Remove the shells and veins from the prawns and wash well. Rub with the mixture of turmeric powder and salt and set aside for 5 minutes.

Heat 2 tablespoons of oil in a pan. Fry 2 prawns and drain. Then fry 2 more prawns. Drain. Add the remaining 1 tablespoon oil. Fry the remaining prawns in the same manner (i.e. 2 at a time). Drain and set aside.

Heat the ghee. Add the cloves, cardamoms and cinnamon. Stir. Add the onion, green chillies and ginger. Stir continuously over a medium flame till the onion becomes light brown in colour. Add the chilli powder and turmeric powder. Stir briefly. Add the curd and stir till the ghee floats. Add the coconut milk, sugar and salt. Bring to a boil. Add the prawns and cook uncovered on a medium flame for about 5 minutes or until the gravy turns moderately thick. Serve hot with rice or puris.

SERVES : 4-6

Doi Murgi
Curd Chicken

It is the incorporation of curd that imparts a unique taste to this dish.
The main accompaniment to this dish is rice or chappatis.

INGREDIENTS

1 medium-sized chicken
(approx 750gms)
3 cups fresh curd
2 tsp turmeric powder   Mix
2 tsp coriander powder   together
2 tsp cummin powder
1 tsp chilli powder
1 cup oil
4 medium-sized onions
(peeled & grated)
1½ tbsp grated ginger
1 tbsp chopped garlic
1 tsp sugar
5 green chillies (chopped)
1 tsp garam masala
2 tsp melted ghee
Salt to taste

METHOD

Cut the chicken into medium–sized pieces. Wash and rub with the curd-masala mixture. Set aside for 30 minutes.

Heat the oil in a pan. Add the onion, ginger, garlic, sugar and green chillies. Fry on a high flame, stirring continuously, for about 3 minutes or until the onion becomes light brown In colour and oil floats on top. Add the chicken along with the curd-masala mixture. Cook uncovered on a high flame for 3 minutes, stirring continuously. Then cook covered over a low flame for about 15 minutes, stirring a few times in-between. When the chicken is almost cooked, add the salt. Cover and cook for 5 minutes or until done. Add the garam masala and ghee. Serve hot with rice or chappatis.

SERVES : 4-6

Katla Machh Kalai
Trout Fish Curry

Although a number of ingredients are used to flavour this popular fish curry, it is indeed very simple to prepare. The main accompaniment to this dish is rice.

INGREDIENTS

500 gms Katla fish (cut into 8-10 pieces)
4 small-sized potatoes
(peeled & cut into 2 pieces each)
Mustard oil for deep frying
2 Bay leaves
1 tsp cummin seeds
1 whole red chilli (broken into 2 pieces)
A pinch asafoetida
2 medium-sized onions ⎤
1" piece ginger   ⎬ Grind to a paste
4 cloves garlic   ⎦
1 medium-sized tomato (chopped)
4 green chillies (stalks removed & kept whole)
½ tsp turmeric powder
½ tsp coriander powder
½ tsp cummin powder
½ tsp chilli powder
½ tsp sugar
1½ cups water
2 tsp melted ghee
2 cloves   ⎤
1"piece cinnamon ⎬ Grind to a powder
2 cardamoms   ⎦
Salt to taste

To Rub On The Fish Pieces
½ tsp turmeric powder
Salt to taste

METHOD

Wash the pieces of fish and rub with the mixture of turmeric powder and salt. Set aside for about 15 minutes. Heat the oil and add a pinch of salt to it, as this will prevent the fish from sticking to the pan while frying. When the oil becomes hot, deep fry the fish pieces 2 or 3 at a time. Drain. Fry the potatoes in the same oil. Drain when brown in colour. Set aside the fried fish and fried potatoes.

In another pan, heat 2 tablespoons oil and put in the whole red chillie, asafoetida, Bay leaves and cummin seeds. Stir. Now add the ground paste, tomato, whole green chillies, turmeric powder, coriander powder, cummin powder, chilli powder and sugar. Fry for 2 minutes. Add the water and bring to a boil. Reduce flame to medium and add the potatoes. Cook uncovered for about 3 minutes. Add the pieces of fish and the salt. Cook uncovered over a medium flame for about 5 minutes, by which time the gravy will be quite thick. Remove the pan from the flame and add the melted ghee and powdered cloves, cinnamon and cardamoms.

Serve hot with rice.

SERVES : 4-6

Lau Chingri

Bottle Gourd with Shrimps

*An excellent way to combine shrimps with vegetables,
to create an unusual taste. The main accompaniment
to this dish is rice or chappatis.*

INGREDIENTS

750 gms bottle gourd (lauki)
1 large potato(peeled & cut into small pieces)
2 cups shelled and washed shrimps
2 tbsp oil
1 tsp cummin seeds
1 Kashmiri chilli (broken into two
through the centre)
1 Bay leaf
1 tsp turmeric powder
2 tsp cummin powder
1 tbsp jaggery
½ cup water
2 cloves
2 cardamoms   } Grind
1" stick cinnamon   together
                        coarsely
1 tsp melted ghee
Salt to taste

METHOD

Peel and cut the bottle gourd into ½" thick rings. Cut each ring into 2 pieces. Then cut each halved ring into ½" thick slanting pieces. Add the potatoes. Wash the bottle gourd and potato pieces together and set aside.

Add ½ teaspoon turmeric powder and salt to the shrimps. Heat the oil and fry the shrimps until light brown in colour. Drain and set aside. In the same oil, add the cummin seeds, Kashmiri chilli and Bay leaf. Stir. Add the bottle gourd, potato, turmeric powder, cummin powder, jaggery, water and salt. Cook three-fourths covered on a low flame for about 10 minutes or until there is no water left. Add the shrimps. Cook uncovered for 3 minutes, stirring most of the time. Add the coarsely ground cloves, cardamom and cinnamon and ghee. Serve hot with chappatis or rice.

SERVES : 4-6

Machh Paturi

Fish in Banana Leaves

Besides preserving the flavour and valuable nutrients, the banana packets look spectacular. The main accompaniment to this dish is rice or chappatis.

INGREDIENTS

*8 medium-sized pieces of Bhekti fish
2 tbsp mustard seeds
4 green chillies (ground to a fine paste using very little water)
1 tsp turmeric powder
2 tsp chilli powder
1 cup grated coconut
2 tbsp coriander leaves
4 green chillies (slit through the centre into 2 pieces & seeds removed)
1 tbsp mustard oil
8 pieces of banana leaves
(approx 7" x 7" squares)
Salt to taste
8 toothpicks
(Thread to tie the fish packets)*

METHOD

Clean and wash the fish. Score both sides of the fish pieces lightly and set aside.

Combine the mustard-green chilli paste, turmeric powder, chilli powder, grated coconut, coriander leaves, salt and mustard oil. Add the pieces of fish to this mixture. Mix well so that the fish pieces are coated with this mixture.

Wash and wipe the banana leaves. Put 1 fish piece on each leaf, top with 1 piece of slit green chilli, fold on all 4 sides, secure with a toothpick and then tie with thread.

Steam the banana packets in a pressure cooker (i.e. after 1 whistle, switch off the gas). When the banana leaves discolour and the toothpicks come out easily, it means that the fish is done. When the pressure cooker is opened, remove the fish and serve hot as part of a regular meal.

SERVES : 4-6

Pomfret Jhol Tomator Sathe
Pomfret Curry with Tomato

In this preparation, tomatoes are incorporated in the gravy, giving it a bright appearance. While frying the pomfret, add a pinch of salt to the hot oil to prevent the pomfret from sticking to the pan. The main accompaniment to this dish is rice or chappatis.

INGREDIENTS

*2 medium-sized pomfrets
(each cut into 5 pieces)
1 cup oil
2 medium-sized onions
(peeled & chopped)
¼ tsp sugar
4 cloves garlic
2 medium-sized tomatoes (chopped)
4 green chillies (chopped)
1" piece ginger (chopped)
½ tsp turmeric powder
½ cup coriander leaves (chopped)
Salt to taste*

To Rub On The Pomfrets
*½ tsp turmeric powder
Salt to taste*

METHOD

Wash the pieces of pomfret and rub with the mixture of turmeric powder and salt. Set aside for about 15 minutes.

Heat the oil and add a pinch of salt to it, as this will prevent the pomfret from sticking to the pan while frying. When the oil becomes hot, fry the pieces of pomfret 2 or 3 at a time. Drain when light brown in colour. Remove excess oil and retain only 2 tablespoons oil in the pan. Add the onion and sugar. Fry over a low flame, stirring often. When the onion becomes light brown in colour, add the garlic. Stir briefly and add the tomato, green chillies, ginger, turmeric powder and salt. Fry on a low flame for about 3 minutes. When a pleasant aroma emanates, add the pieces of fried pomfret, arranging them in a single layer. Sprinkle the coriander leaves all over the pomfret pieces and cook covered on a low flame for about 3 minutes. Uncover and stir the pomfret pieces very carefully, turning them upside down. Cover and cook on a low flame for about 3 minutes.

Serve hot with chappatis or rice.

SERVES : 4-6

Sarse Ilish

Hilsa Fish in Mustard

As the name implies, the fish is cooked in a mustard-based gravy which gives an extraordinary flavour and taste to this preparation. The main accompaniment to this dish is rice.

INGREDIENTS

*500 gms Hilsa fish
(cut into 10-12 pieces)
1 tsp turmeric powder
2 tsp mustard seeds
4 green chillies
2 tbsp mustard oil
(refined groundnut oil can be used
if preferred but mustard oil lends
a distinctive taste)
1 cup water
Salt to taste*

To Rub On The Fish Pieces
*½ tsp turmeric powder
Salt to taste*

METHOD

Wash the pieces of fish and rub with the mixture of turmeric powder and salt. Set aside for 10-15 minutes. Slit 2 green chillies through their centres but keep whole. Grind together the remaining 2 green chillies and the mustard seeds, using very little water, so as to obtain a thick paste. Add turmeric powder to the paste and set aside.

Heat 1 tablespoon oil in a broad pan and put the pieces of fish into it, in a single layer. Add the whole green chillies, the ground paste, salt and water. Bring to a boil. Cook uncovered on a high flame for 2 minutes. Carefully turn over the fish pieces and cook uncovered on a high flame for 5 minutes. Add the remaining 1 tablespoon oil and cover the pan. Remove from the flame and serve hot with rice.

SERVES : 4-6

Bhappa Doi

Steamed Sweet Curd

A delicacy indeed. This preparation from curd makes an unusual and nourishing dessert–the perfect ending to a meal. For best results, the fresh curd used in this preparation should be made using very good quality whole milk and not skimmed milk.

INGREDIENTS

1 cup fresh curd
½ cup milk
½ tin condensed milk (approx 1 cup)
1 tbsp small pieces of blanched almonds
1 tbsp small pieces of blanched pistachio nuts

METHOD

Combine the curd, milk and condensed milk. Beat with an egg beater or whip in a mixer until smooth. Add the almonds and pistachio nuts. Mix well.

Pour the contents into a pudding bowl. Cover the mouth of the bowl with a piece of newspaper, butterpaper or foil and secure with a rubberband.

Pour 3 cups of water into a pressure cooker. Put the grid in. Place the bowl containing the curd mixture on it. Close the pressure cooker and steam till the curd is well set (i.e. after 1 whistle, pressure cook on a low flame for about 20 minutes).

When the pressure cooker is opened, remove the newspaper covering and cool the set curd at room temperature. After cooling, discard the water, if any, very carefully without disturbing the shape of the curd. Cool in the refrigerator.

Serve cold as a dessert in the same pudding bowl in which the curd was steamed.

SERVES : 4-6

Cholar Dal

Bengal Gram Lentils

An unusual dal preparation, slightly sweet and delicately spiced, contain-
ing coconut, raisins and vegetables. The dal will be appetising both in
appearance and taste if it is not very watery
and if the whole grains of dal are visible. The main
accompaniment to this dish is rice or chappatis.

INGREDIENTS

2 cups Bengal gram (chana dal)
4½ cups water
1 tsp turmeric powder
2 tsp sugar
2 tsp melted ghee or oil
2 Bay leaves
2 cloves
2 small sticks cinnamon
2 cardamoms
½ tsp cummin seeds
½ cup coconut pieces
(thin ¼" x ¼" slices)
2 tbsp raisins
1 tsp chilli powder
1 medium-sized potato
(peeled & cut into 12 pieces)
1 cup medium-sized pieces of cauliflower
Oil for deep frying
Salt to taste

METHOD

Heat the oil for deep frying. Deep fry the potatoes and cauliflower separately. Drain when light brown in colour and set aside.

Pick, wash and soak the in 4 cups water for about 30 minutes. Cook in the pressure cooker till the dal is soft but not overcooked. Each grain of dal should be visible. When the pressure cooker is opened, add the turmeric powder, salt and sugar.

In a separate pan, heat 2 tablespoons oil and add the Bay leaves, cloves, cinnamon, cardamoms, cummin seeds, coconut, raisins and chilli powder. Stir briefly. Add the cooked dal and ½ cup water. Bring to a boil. Add the fried potatoes and cauliflower and cook on a low flame, without covering, for about 3 minutes, stirring once, until the dal is quite thick. Serve hot with chappatis or rice.

SERVES : 4-6

Dhokar Dalna

Lentil Pieces in Gravy

A tasty preparation, slightly time-consuming but worth the trouble.
The main accompaniment to this dish is rice or chappatis.

INGREDIENTS

1½ cups Bengal gram (chana dal)
½ cup oil
½ tsp turmeric powder
1 whole red chilli   ⎤ roast
1 tsp cummin seeds   ⎬ without
1 tsp sugar   ⎦ oil and
                        grind
2 medium-sized potatoes
(peeled & cut into small pieces)
Oil for deep frying
Salt to taste

For The Gravy
2 tbsp oil
1 tsp cummin seeds
2 Bay leaves
1 red chilli
1" piece ginger (ground)
¾ tsp turmeric powder
1 tsp cummin seed powder
1 tsp chilli powder
1 tsp sugar
3 cups water
1 tsp melted ghee
1/2 tsp garam masala
Salt to taste

METHOD

Pick, wash and soak the dal in water either overnight or for at least 4 hours. Drain and grind coarsely.

Heat ½ cup oil, reduce flame and add the ground dal. Then add the turmeric powder, red chilli-cummin powder, sugar and salt. Sauté uncovered for 5-7 minutes, stirring often. Remove from the flame. Grease a high-edged steel plate (thali) and spread the dal all over it to a thickness of ½". Make the surface smooth with a flat knife. Allow it to cool and then cut into 1½" X 1½" sized diamond-shaped pieces. Set aside.

Heat the oil for deep frying. When it starts smoking, add the chopped dal pieces, a few at a time. Drain when golden. In the same oil, deep fry the potatoes until light brown in colour. Drain and set aside.

In a separate pan, heat 2 tablespoons oil and add the cummin seeds, Bay leaves and red chilli, Fry briefly. Add the ginger, turmeric powder, cummin powder, chilli powder and sugar and fry for 2 minutes. Add the water and when it boils, add the potatoes. Cook covered on a low flame for 3 minutes. Add salt and stir. Very carefully add the fried dal pieces which are called `dhoka'. Cook uncovered on a high flame for 3 minutes. Remove from heat. Add ghee and garam masala. Cover. Serve hot with rice or chappatis.

SERVES : 4-6

Sarse Dharosh

Lady's Fingers in Mustard

Lady's Fingers are cooked in a mustard-based gravy, which makes this dish not only delectable but also unique. Handle the lady's fingers with a delicate touch and also ensure that they are not over-cooked because broken pieces of lady's fingers will make the dish unsightly and tasteless. The main accompaniment to this dish is chappatis.

INGREDIENTS

50 medium & equal-sized lady's fingers
2 tbsp oil
½ tsp mustard seeds
1 tsp poppy seeds
1 tsp mustard seeds
2 green chillies
¼ tsp turmeric powder
¼ cup water
Salt to taste

Grind to a paste using little water

METHOD

Wash the lady's fingers. Wipe dry with a clean napkin. Trim both ends, slit on one side almost all the way, keeping the lady's fingers intact. Set aside.

Heat the oil in a pan. Add the mustard seeds. When they splutter, add the lady's fingers and fry uncovered on a high flame for about 2 minutes, stirring continuously. Add the ground paste, turmeric powder and salt. Stir. Add the water. Cook covered on a low flame for 5 minutes, stirring twice in-between. Then cook uncovered on a high flame for 3 minutes, stirring twice carefully, so that the lady's fingers do not break.

Serve hot with chappatis.

SERVES : 4-6

Shukto

Mixed Vegetable Curry

Besides providing an opportunity to pick and choose the preferred vegetables when eating, this dish is most aromatic and contains bitter gourd too, which helps in digesting the food. The main accompaniment to this dish is rice.

INGREDIENTS

1 medium-sized potato
(peeled & cut into ½" long thick, pieces)
2 medium-sized bitter gourds
(scraped and cut into ½" long thick pieces)
1 raw banana (peeled & cut into 6 pieces)
1 sweet potato (washed & cut into 6 pieces)
1 medium-sized brinjal
(cut into ½" thick long pieces)
1 2 drumsticks (3" long each)
3 tbsp oil
6 urad dal wadis (fried)
1 Bay leaf
1 red chilli (broken into 2 pieces)
A pinch of asafoetida
½ tsp panch phoron(mixture of cummin seeds,
mustard seeds, fenugreek seeds, aniseeds &
onion seeds)
½ tsp turmeric powder
½ tsp cummin powder
½ coriander powder
½ tsp sugar
2 cups water
½ cup milk
1 tsp panch phoron powder (obtained by
grinding together equal quantities of cummin
seeds, mustards seeds, fenugreek seeds,
aniseeds and onion seeds)
Salt to taste

METHOD

Wash all the vegetables together. Heat the oil in a pan. Add the Bay leaf, red chilli, asafoetlda and panch phoron. Fry all these briskly. Add the vegetables, turmeric powder, cummin powder, coriander powder and sugar. Fry on a high flame for 3 minutes, stirring continuously. Add the wadis, water and salt. Bring to a boil. Cook half-covered on a low flame for about 15 minutes or until the vegetables become soft and very little gravy is left. Add the milk and cook uncovered for 3 minutes. Sprinkle the panch phoron powder on top. Do not stir. Serve hot with rice.

SERVES : 4-6

Goan

Chicken Xacuti

Pieces of chicken are cooked in a gravy containing an array of spices and pieces of coconut. This mouth-watering dish is usually served at weddings and parties. The main accompaniment to this dish is rice or bread or chappatis.

INGREDIENTS

1 tender fresh chicken (approx 750 gms)
¾ cup dry white gram or dry green peas
6 tbsp oil
1 small onion (peeled & cut into long thin slices)
¼ coconut (cut into ½" x ½" sized thin pieces)
1 cup water
¼ cup thick tamarind juice
Salt to taste

For The Masala
2 tsp coriander seeds
2 tsp cummin seeds
1 tsp aniseeds
½" piece turmeric
6 Kashmiri chillies
4 peppercorns
3 cloves
½" piece cinnamon
3 cardamoms
¾ tsp poppy seeds
A small piece of nutmeg (optional)
1 medium-sized onion
(peeled & cut into small pieces)
4 cloves garlic (peeled)
½" piece ginger(scraped)
¼ cup fresh grated coconut
1 cup water (for grinding masala)

METHOD

Cut the chicken into medium-sized pieces, wash well and set aside.

Soak the dry white gram or dry green peas in water overnight. Add salt and pressure cook until soft but not mashed. Retain only ¼ cup water in the boiled white gram or green peas and discard the excess water. Set aside. Roast all the items under masala, in a dry pan (i.e. without using oil), for about 5 minutes, over a medium flame. Cool slightly and grind finely using water a little at a time. The total amount of water used should be 1 cup. Now pass the ground masala through a sieve, in order to separate the masala and the masala water. Set both aside separately.

Heat the oil and add the long thin sliced onion. Fry on a low flame, stirring often, until the onion becomes light brown in colour. Add the ground masala and fry on a low flame for about 5 minutes, stirring often. Add the chicken pieces and fry over a medium flame for about 7-10 minutes, stirring often. Add the coconut pieces, tamarind juice, masala water, water and salt. Bring to a boil. Cook covered on a low flame for about 20 minutes, stirring occasionally. When the chicken is cooked, add the boiled gram or peas and cook uncovered on a high flame for about 3 minutes. Serve hot with rice, bread or chappatis.

SERVES : 4-6

Mutton Chops

This is a popular and delicious side dish. Flattening the chops is a must because this helps the masala to penetrate into the meat.

INGREDIENTS

*600 gms mutton chops
(approx 8-10 medium-sized chops)
6 green chillies
6 cloves garlic
1" piece ginger
1 tbsp garam masala
½ tsp turmeric powder
juice of 2 medium-sized lemons
6 eggs
6 tbsp semolina
Oil for frying
Salt to taste*

METHOD

Wash the chops well with water and flatten them with a mallet or grinding stone.

Add very little water and pressure cook the chops until tender but not overcooked. When the cooker is opened, remove the chops and cool at room temperature, making sure that no water clings to the chops.

Combine the green chillies, garlic, ginger and grind to a fine paste. Add the garam masala, turmeric powder, lemon juice and salt, to this paste. Rub the resulting masala on the chops and set them aside for about 30 minutes.

Add a little salt to the eggs and beat well. Roll the chops one by one in semolina and then in the beaten eggs and shallow fry the chops either in a flat frying pan, tawa or nonstick pan, using a little oil. Drain the chops when both sides become golden brown.

Serve hot as a side dish.

SERVES : 4-6

Pork Vindaloo

One of the most famous Goan curries–deliciously hot and sour.
This dish is considered a delicacy and served at weddings and parties.
The main accompaniment to this dish is bread.

INGREDIENTS

600 gms lean pork
12 cloves garlic
8 Kashmiri chillies
2 tsp cummin seeds ⎱ Grind
8 peppercorns ⎰ together to a fine
½ tsp turmeric powder paste
¼ cup vinegar
¼ cup water
¾ cup vinegar
½ cup water
Salt to taste

METHOD

Mix the ground paste with ¾ cup vinegar and ½ cup water. Set aside.

Cut the pork into 4" squares and wash well. Drain water thoroughly and wipe the pork pieces with a clean cloth. Mix together the pork pieces, ground paste and salt. Set aside for about 1 hour.

After 1 hour, put all the ingredients in a pan and bring to a boil. Reduce flame and cook partly covered for about 20 minutes or till the pork is tender, and the gravy thick. Remove the pork pieces from the gravy and cut into 4" x ½" pieces. Put the pieces back into the gravy.

Serve hot or cold (room temperature) with bread or as a side dish. Pork Vindaloo can also be served as a cocktail snack, in which case no gravy is needed. The leftover gravy can be evaporated by cooking on a high flame for a few minutes.

SERVES : 4-6

Prawn Curry

This is another popular curry using ground masala prepared from coconut along with other spices. Nothing is more satisfying and enjoyable than a combination of this curry and rice. The main accompaniment to this dish is either rice, bread or chappatis.

INGREDIENTS

1½ cups shelled and deveined big white prawns

1 cup grated coconut	Grind
2 tsp coriander seeds	using
3 tsp chilli powder	1 cup of
½ tsp turmeric powder	water a little at a
4 peppercorns	time

3 medium-sized tomatoes (cut into small pieces)
3 green chillies (cut through the centre
& kept whole)
⅓ cup tamarind juice
1 ½ cups water
4 tbsp oil
Salt to taste

METHOD

Wash the prawns, add a little salt and set aside for about 10 minutes. Put the prawns in a pan, discarding the salt water.

Pass the ground masala through a sieve, so as to separate the masala and the masala water. Keep both separate.

Heat the oil in a pan and add the ground masala and the prawns. Mix well. Add the masala water, tomatoes, green chillies, tamarind juice, water and salt. Bring to a boil. Cook partly covered on a low flame for about 10 minutes, stirring occasionally. Serve hot with rice, bread or chappatis.

SERVES : 4-6

Prawn Pulao

An exotic looking pulao makes a meal all the more enjoyable while providing proper sustenance. The sugar must be added only at the frying stage as this helps to darken the colour.

INGREDIENTS

2 cups rice
3 tbsp oil
1 large onion (peeled & chopped)
1 tsp sugar
1" piece cinnamon
3 cardamoms
4 cloves
8 peppercorns
4 medium-sized tomatoes (chopped)
¾ cup prawns (shelled & deveined)
3¾ cups water
Salt to taste

For Garnishing
2 hardboiled eggs (shelled & cut into halves)
1 tbsp chopped coriander leaves

METHOD

Pick, wash and soak the rice in water for 30 minutes.

Heat the oil in a pan. Add the onion and fry over a low flame for a few minutes, stirring often. When the onion turns brown, add the sugar, cinnamon, cardamoms, cloves and peppercorns. Stir briefly. Add the drained rice, tomatoes and prawns. Fry on a medium flame for about 5 minutes, stirring most of the time. Add the water and salt. Bring to a boil. Cook covered on a low flame until the rice is ready, stirring a few times in-between.

Transfer the hot rice into an attractive serving dish. Top with the halved hardboiled eggs. Put some coriander leaves on the eggs.

Bengal Gram

A good source of protein. The ground paste of coconut and the spices add flavour and taste to the dish. The main accompaniment is bread or chappatis.

INGREDIENTS

1 cup Bengal gram(chana dal)
2 ½ cups water
2 tbsp oil
8 cloves garlic (peeled & crushed)
1 cup grated coconut ⎤
8 peppercorns ⎟ Grind to
6 red chillies ⎬ a fine
½ tsp turmeric powder ⎟ paste
¼ cup water ⎦
2 tbsp chopped coriander leaves
Salt to taste

METHOD

Pick, wash and soak the dal in 2½ cups water for about 30 minutes.

Pass the ground masala through a sieve, so as to separate the masala and masala water. Keep both separate.

Heat the oil in a pan. Add the garlic and fry until slightly brown in colour. Add the ground masala and fry on a low flame for 5 minutes, stirring often. Add the dal along with the water in which it was soaked, the masala water and salt. Pressure cook the dal till done i.e. after one whistle, pressure cook on a low flame for about 3 minutes. When the pressure cooker is opened, cook uncovered on a low flame for about 3 minutes. Garnish with coriander leaves. Serve hot with bread or chappatis.

SERVES : 4-6

Crescents

These are beautiful crescent shaped biscuits with cashewnuts.
The main accompaniment to this dish is tea or coffee.

INGREDIENTS

½ cup refined flour (maida)
A pinch of soda bicarbonate
A pinch of salt
2 tbsp powdered cashewnuts
2 tbsp powdered sugar
3 tbsp melted ghee
1 tbsp milk
¼ tsp vanilla essence

For Sprinkling On Top
2 tbsp sifted icing sugar

METHODS

Sieve together the refined flour, soda bi carbonate and salt. Add the cashewnuts and set aside.

Cream together the sugar and ghee. Add the milk and vanilla essence and mix well. Add the flour to this mixture and knead well, so as to obtain a pliable dough.

Divide the dough into 4 parts. On a lightly floured surface, form each part of the dough into a roll as thick as a pencil. Then cut into 1½" lengths, taper the ends and curve into crescent shapes. Arrange these crescents 1" apart on a lightly greased baking tray. Bake in the centre of a preheated moderate oven at 350° F for about 20-25 minutes or until light brown and firm. Remove from the oven and cool in the tray for a minute. Remove from the tray and sprinkle sifted icing sugar while the crescents are still warm. Cool thoroughly and store in an airtight container.

Serve as a tea-time snack or tidbit during Christmas.

SERVES : 4-6

Eggless Cake

A cake is always welcome and more so this eggless cake, which can satisfy even strict vegetarians. This cake can also be served during Christmas or on any other occasion. To get more butter from cream, thick cream is required. To achieve this, place the pan containing milk in the refrigerator while the milk is slightly warm. The main accompaniment to this dish is tea or coffee.

INGREDIENTS

1½ cups refined flour (maida)
1¾ tsp soda bi carbonate
1¾ tsp baking powder
¾ cup saltless white butter*
1 tin condensed milk
½ cup cold milk

For The Topping
½ cup sifted icing sugar

METHODS

Sieve the refined flour, soda bi carbonate and baking powder together.

Melt the butter in a saucepan over a low flame for about a minute. Remove the pan from the flame. Add the condensed milk and stir for 2 minutes. Add the sieved flour and stir for about 2 minutes. Add the milk and mix well, stirring for another 2 minutes.

Grease and dust the base and sides of an 8" diameter cake tin. Pour the prepared mixture into it. Bake in a preheated moderate oven i.e. 350ºF for 45 minutes or till golden brown in colour. Remove from the oven immediately. Cool at room temperature in the tin. Remove from the tin and dust with icing sugar. Cut into 2" x 1½" pieces. Store in an airtight container at room temperature.

Serve as a tea-time snack or tidbit on feste days.

* White butter is available in a number of shops. However, this can be easily made at home too. Collect cream from the top of milk which has been boiled and kept on the refrigerator shelf. After collecting the cream for about 5 days, add some chilled water and run in the mixer for about 3-5 minutes, by which time the butter will rise to the surface. Remove the butter and discard the water. It is not advisable to use very old cream.

SERVES : 4-6

GOAN

Nankhatai
Baked Delight

A perennial baked favourite, which can be served at any time.
However, it is also served during Christmas along with other sweets.
The main accompaniment to this dish is tea or coffee.

INGREDIENTS

2 cups refined flour
1 tsp soda bi carbonate
²/₃ cup powdered sugar
¾ cup melted ghee
4 finely powdered cardamoms
7 pistachio nuts (cut into long thin pieces
without peeling)

METHODS

Sieve together the refined flour, soda bicarbonate and sugar. Add the ghee and cardamoms and prepare a smooth dough.

Divide the dough into 22 portions and form round balls. Flatten the balls a little at the base. Press a few pistachio nuts lightly into the centre of each ball. Arrange the balls in two flat ungreased baking trays, leaving 1" space between each ball. Bake in a preheated moderate oven at 350° for about 40 minutes or until light brown in colour. Remove from the oven and cool in the trays. Remove from the trays and cool again. Then store in an airtight container.

Serve as a tea-time snack or as a tidbit on festival days.

Gujarati

Amiri Khaman

Lentil Crumbs

This attractive looking concoction enables you to enjoy a combination of soft and crunchy tastes. It forms an ideal snack or side dish for any occasion. After adding the sev just before serving, do not cover this dish, as the sev will then lose its crunchiness.

INGREDIENTS

2 cups Bengal gram
2 tbsp sour curd or
3 tbsp fresh curd   ⎫ Grind
8 green chillies   ⎬ to a
1" piece ginger   ⎭ paste
¼ tsp turmeric powder
¼ tsp soda bi carbonate
1 tsp sugar
Juice of a medium-sized lemon
Salt to taste

For The Vaghar
2 tbsp oil
1 tsp mustard seeds
8 cloves garlic (peeled & coarsely crushed)
A big pinch of asafoetida

For Garnishing
¼ cup grated coconut
3 tbsp chopped coriander leaves
1 ½ cups fine sev

METHOD

Pick, wash and soak the dal in water for about 6 hours. Drain and grind coarsely to form a thick mixture. Add the curd and set aside for about 4 hours to ferment.

After fermentation, add the ground green chilli-ginger paste, turmeric powder, salt and soda bi carbonate. Spread this mixture in a greased thali with high edges. Steam for about 20 minutes. Test by piercing with a knife, which should come out clean. Cool the cooked mixture.

Remove from the thali using a knife and crumble by hand. Add the sugar and lemon juice. Mix well.

Heat the oil. Add the mustard seeds. When they splutter, add the garlic. Fry briefly and add the asafoetida. Pour this mixture on the crumbled mixture. Mix well. Cover and set aside at room temperature till you are ready to serve. Just before serving, garnish with the coconut, coriander leaves and sev.

Serve as a snack or as a side dish to a meal.

SERVES : 4-6

Dahi Kadhi
Curd Curry

A traditional mouth-watering dish served at weddings and other functions. It is such a favourite that it is popular even for day-to-day cooking. It is best enjoyed with plain boiled rice. When the curry starts boiling, stir continuously for the first few minutes, as at this stage, it is likely to bubble up and may oveflow. The main accompaniment to this is rice, khichri or pulao

INGREDIENTS

1 ½ cups thick slightly sour curd
2 tbsp gram flour
5 cups water
20 curry leaves
1 tsp green chillies (chopped)
1 ½ tsp chopped ginger
½ cup small pieces of white radish (optional)
1 ½ tsp sugar
2 tbsp chopped coriander leaves
Salt to taste

For The Vaghar
1 ½ tbsp oil
2 red chillies
$1/3$ tsp mustard seeds
$1/3$ tsp fenugreek seeds
$1/3$ tsp cummin seeds
4 cloves
A big pinch of asafoetida

METHOD

Combine the curd, gram flour and ½ cup water in a pan. Beat well with an egg beater and prepare a smooth batter. Add the remaining 4½ cups water, curry leaves, green chillies, ginger, white radish, sugar and salt. Set aside.

Heat the oil and add the red chillies, mustard seeds and fenugreek seeds. When these start spluttering, remove the pan from the flame and immediately add the cummin seeds, cloves and asafoetida. Place the pan on the flame, stir quickly and add the prepared curd mixture. Bring to a boil, reduce flame and stir almost continuously, as at this stage, the curry has a tendency to bubble up. When the bubbling stops, cook uncovered for about 10 minutes on a medium flame, stirring occasionally. Garnish with coriander leaves.

Serve hot with rice, khichri or pulao.

SERVES : 4-6

Dal Dhokli

Sour Chappati Squares in Dal

Small pieces of rolled chappati dough are cooked in a sweet and sour dal. An excellent meal-in-a dish. After adding the dhoklis, stir the dal often so that the dhoklis do not stick to the bottom of the pan. The main accompaniment to this dish is rice.

INGREDIENTS

For The Dal
¾ cup toovar dal
4 ½ cups water
½ tsp turmeric powder
20 curry leaves
2 tbsp jaggery
2 tsp thick tamarind juice
4 tbsp chopped coriander leaves
Salt to taste

For The Vaghar
2 tbsp oil
A big pinch asafoetida
½ tsp mustard seeds
½ tsp cummin seeds
½" piece ginger
6 cloves garlic (optional)
5 green chillies

For The Dhoklis
1½ cups wheat flour
1 tsp ajwain (optional)
¼ tsp cummin seeds
¼ tsp turmeric powder
½ tsp chilli powder
Very little water
1 tbsp oil
Salt to taste

METHOD

First prepare the dhoklis. Combine all the ingredients mentioned under dhoklis, with the exception of oil and water. Add oil and rub in with the fingers, till the mixture resembles bread crumbs. Add water little by little and prepare a stiff dough. Divide the dough into 4 equal parts and roll each part as thin as a chappati. Cut into 1" x 1" squares. Set aside.

Pick, wash and soak the dal in 2 cups water for 30 minutes. Pressure cook till the dal becomes quite soft. When the pressure cooker is opened, mash the dal with an egg beater or wooden churner. Add the turmeric powder, salt, curry leaves and the remaining 2½ cups water. Bring to a boil. Add the jaggery and tamarind juice.

Heat 2 tablespoons oil separately. Add the asafoetida, mustard seeds, cummin seeds and the ground paste. When the mustard seeds splutter, add all these ingredients to the prepared dal. Stir and add the dhokli pieces to the dal. Cook uncovered on a low flame for about 10 minutes, stirring 4 to 5 times, very carefully, so that the dhokli pieces do not stick to the bottom of the pan and each piece of dhokli is separate. Garnish with chopped coriander leaves.

Serve hot as a-meal-in-a-dish.

SERVES : 4-6

Gor Papdi
Wheat and Jaggery Squares

A delicately flavoured nutritious sweet–jaggery being a good source of iron. This sweet can be prepared on any occasion including festivals like Diwali.

INGREDIENTS

½ cup melted ghee
1 cup wheat flour
1 tsp aniseeds (optional)
A pinch of nutmeg powder
or 2 crushed cardamoms

For The Syrup
1 tsp melted ghee
¾ cup jaggery

METHOD

Heat the ghee. Add the wheat flour and aniseeds. Fry over a medium flame for about 5 minutes, stirring continuously. When the flour becomes light brown in colour, remove from the flame and cool at room temperature.

Next prepare the syrup. Heat the ghee and jaggery together in a thick-bottomed pan and cook over a low flame, stirring most of the time, for about 3 minutes. When the jaggery melts, add the fried flour and nutmeg or cardamoms. Stir continuously until everything is well mixed. Pour the mixture into a greased thali to a thickness of about ½". Mark 1"x1" squares with a sharp knife, immediately. Remove the pieces carefully with a flat spatula when the mixture is cold. Store in an airtight container.

Serve as a sweet during festivals or along with a meal.

MAKE : 10 PIECES

Handuo

Spicy Cake

This delicious spicy cake makes an uncommon snack and is suitable for special occasions too. The main accompaniment to this dish is hot mango pickle chunda pickle or coriander chutney.

INGREDIENTS

1 cup rice
½ cup white urad dal
½ Bengal gram
½ cup sour curd or
¾ cup fresh curd
1 cup grated bottle gourd or
¾ cup shelled green peas
6 green chillies
1" piece ginger
½ tsp soda bi carbonate
2 tsp sugar
¼ tsp turmeric powder
½ tsp chilli powder
Juice of a small lemon
4 tbsp oil
Salt to taste

For the Vaghar
4 tbsp oil
1 tsp mustard seeds
1 tsp seasame seeds
¼ tsp asafoetida

METHOD

Combine the rice, urad dal and Bengal gram. Dry grind to a coarse mixture somewhat similar to semolina. Soak the rice and dals together in water overnight and grind to a coarse mixture the next day. Add the curd and sufficient hot water so as to prepare a thick batter. Cover and set aside for about 8 hours for fermentation.

After fermentation, add the bottle gourd, or green peas, green chilli-ginger paste, soda bi carbonate, sugar, tumeric powder, chilli powder, salt, lemon juice and oil to the batter. Mix well. Spread this mixture in a greased thali with high edges, making a thin layer. Heat the oil mentioned under Vaghar. Add the mustard seeds, sesame seeds and asafoetida. Stir and pour quickly all over the surface of the batter. Do not mix.

Bake this batter in a preheated oven at 350° F for 40 minutes or until the crust is brown. Also, test by inserting a knife, which should come out clean. If you wish, you can prepare this cake without an oven. For this, pour the batter into a thick pan and cover it with a big thali. Cook on a medium flame for 10-15 minutes. Then turn over and cook the other side for 10-15 minutes.

Cut into slices and serve hot as a snack or side dish to a meal with coriander chutney or hot pickle.

SERVES : 4-6

Khakhara

Thin Crispy Chappatis

A non-spicy evergreen snack which can be served at any time of the day. The biggest advantage is that it can be preserved for several days. The main accompaniment to this dish is tea, or the masala from ready pickle spices mixed with a little oil.

INGREDIENTS

2 cups wheat flour
2 tbsp oil
Water
Ghee
Salt to taste

METHOD

Combine the flour and salt. Mix well and then add the oil and rub with the fingers. Add water little by little and prepare a dough similar to that for chappatis. Knead well. Make small balls from the dough and roll into very thin discs (somewhat similar to the thickness of papads), about 7" in diameter. Heat a griddle (tawa) and cook all the discs one by one just like chappatis without applying oil. Set aside.

Put a few drops of ghee on the hot tawa. Keep the flame low and put one chappati on it. Press the chappati with a clean napkin, rotating it clockwise. When the underside becomes crisp, turn over and cook in the same manner until the other side also becomes crisp. Repeat with the remaining chappatis. When all the Khakharas are ready, cool them thoroughly at room temperature. Store in an airtight contaner. These Khakharas can be preserved outside the refrigerator for several days.

Serve as a snack, with or without masala removed from any ready pickle, preferably mango pickle.

To save time, several Khakharas can be piled up on a tawa and then made crisp.

SERVES : 4-6

Kela Nu Raita

Curd Sauce with Bananas

*An unusual sweet and sour accompaniment to a meal
with the latent taste of mustard.*

INGREDIENTS

1 ½ cups fresh curd
¼ cup water
1 tsp green chilli paste
1 tsp mustard powder
1 tsp sugar
2 medium–sized ripe bananas
¼ cup chopped coriander leaves
Salt to taste

METHOD

Beat the curd wth an egg beater so as to make it absolutely smooth. Add the water, green chilli paste, mustard powder, sugar and salt. Beat once again.

Peel and then chop the bananas into ½" cubes. Add immediately to the prepared curd mixture. Mix well. Garnish with coriander leaves. Chill on the refrigerator shelf.

Serve cold as an accompaniment to any meal.

SERVES : 4-6

Khandvi

Gram Flour-Curd Snack

An interesting snack with a yellow, soft look. It can be served on any occasion or as a side dish to a meal. The main accompaniment to this dish is coriander chutney.

INGREDIENTS

¾ cup gram flour
¾ cup sour curd (beaten)
1 ½ cups water ⎤
2 green chillies ⎬ Grind to a paste
½" piece ginger ⎦
¼ tsp turmeric powder
A big pinch of asafoetida
1 tsp oil
Salt to taste

For the Vaghar
2 tbsp oil
1 tsp mustard seeds
A pinch of asafoetida

For Garnishing
¼ cup grated coconut
¼ cup chopped coriander leaves

METHOD

Combine the gram flour, curd and water. Blend, making sure there are absolutely no lumps. Add the green chilli–ginger paste, turmeric powder, asafoetida and salt. Mix well.

Pour this mixture into a pan. Cook uncovered on a low flame, stirring constantly, until thick. Add a teaspoon of oil and mix well. Test by spreading a teaspoon of the mixture on the back of a thali. If it comes off easily, it means that the consistency is right. If the consistency is not proper, cook for a few minutes longer and test again.

When the right consistency is achieved, quickly spread the mixture thinly on the back of a thali or any flat working surface. Cool at room temperature. Cut the spread mixtue into 1" broad strips and roll up one by one. Arrange the rolls in a single layer in a flat serving dish.

Heat the oil. Add the mustard seeds. When they splutter, add the asafoetida and pour this mixture on the Khandvi rolls. Garnish with coconut and coriander leaves.

Serve as a snack accompanied with green coriander chutney.

SERVES : 4-6

Sem Nu Shaak
Broad Beans Vegetable

This is a vegetable dish low on fat and spice and high in roughage, the latter being excellent for health. Moreover, it is quick and easy to prepare. Do not make the mistake of adding water to this vegetable, as this will spoil the taste. The main accompaniment to this dish is chappatis.

INGREDIENTS

400 gms broad beans (sem)
4 small brinjals
1 big potato
1 tbsp oil
½ tsp mustard seeds
A pinch of asafoetida
1 tbsp big pieces of green chillies
1 tsp chopped ginger
1 tsp sugar
½ tsp turmeric powder
½ tsp chilli powder
2 tsp coriander powder
1 tsp cummin powder
Salt to taste

METHOD

String and cut the broad beans into ¾" long pieces. Trim and cut each brinjal into 8 pieces. Peel the potato and cut into small pieces. Wash all the vegetables together. Set aside.

Heat the oil in a pan. Add the mustard seeds. When they splutter, add the asafoetida, green chillies, ginger and sugar. Stir. Add the vegetables, turmeric powder, chilli powder, coriander powder, cummin powder and salt. Stir on a high flame for 2 minutes. Cook covered on a low flame for about 15 minutes or until the vegetables are cooked. Stir 3 or 4 times in–between. Cook uncovered on a high flame for a minute, stirring continuously.

Serve hot with chappatis.

SERVES : 4-6

Undhia
Mixed Vegetables

One of the best Gujarati dishes. Usually served at weddings and other functions. It is so popular that it is specially reserved for Sunday lunch during the winter months, when most vegetables are easily available. In order to obtain an oily look without using too much oil, make sure the water is added immediately after the mustard seeds splutter and not after putting in the vegetables. The main accompaniment to this dish is puris.

INGREDIENTS

2 ¾ cups tender small papri (200 gms)
6 medium-sized pieces kandh (200 gms)
6 small brinjals
4 small potatoes
1 medium-sized sweet potato (optional)
1 medium-sized raw banana (optional)
½ cup shelled green peas or
½ cup fresh tooar seeds

For the Masala
½ tsp asafoetida
2 tsp coriander-cummin powder
1 tsp garam masala
¼ cup jaggery
1 tsp seasame seeds
8 green chillies
1" piece ginger
2 cups coriander leaves
1½ cups grated coconut
4 tbsp oil
Salt to taste

For The Vaghar
½ cup oil
¼ tsp asafoetida

¾ tsp mustard seeds
3 cups water

For the Muthias
¾ cup gram flour
¼ cup wheat flour
½ cup chopped methi leaves
¼ tsp turmeric powder
¼ tsp chilli powder
¼ tsp garam masala
1 tbsp oil
A little water (if required)
Oil for deep frying
Salt to taste

METHOD

First prepare the muthias. Combine all the ingredients mentioned under Muthias except water and the oil for deep frying. Add very little water and prepare a stiff dough. Make small lemon–sized balls from the dough. Heat oil in a pan and deep fry the balls over a medium flame until golden brown on all sides. Drain and set aside.

SERVES : 4-6

String the papris and split into two. Peel and cut the kandh into medium-sized pieces. Peel the potatoes. Slit the peeled potatoes and the brinjals into fours, keeping the base intact. Cut the sweet potato and raw banana, without peeling, into 4 pieces each. Wash all the vegetables separately and set aside.

Mix all the ingredients mentioned under Masala. Stuff the potatoes and brinjals with this masala. Rub the same masala on all the other vegetables separately. Heat the ½ cup oil mentioned under Vaghar, in a thick, broad pan. Add the asafoetida and mustard seeds.

When the mustard seeds splutter, add 3 cups water. Bring to a boil. Reduce flame and arrange all the vegetables in layers. First arrange the papris and green peas or toovar seeds. Next arrange the kandh, followed by the potatoes, brinjals, sweet potatoes and raw bananas. Cook covered on a low flame for about 30 minutes, stirring 3 or 4 times very carefully, so that the vegetables are not mashed. Now arrange the fried muthias on top of the vegetables and cook covered on a low flame for about 5 minutes or until the vegetables are cooked. However, make sure the Undhia is not very dry but has just a little gravy.

Serve hot with hot puris.

Hyderabadi

Murg Biryani
Chicken Biryani

*The very name is enough to tickle the appetite. Unbelievably
delicious and aromatic and consequently irresistible when it is
served at weddings and festivals such as Id. The main accompaniments
to this dish are Burhaani raita or vegetable raita.*

INGREDIENTS

For The Chicken
350 gms chicken (cut into medium-sized pieces)
¼ cup water
2 cups oil
2 cups chopped onion
Salt to taste

For The Marinade
2 green chillies
½ cup coriander leaves
1 tbsp ginger   A
¾ tbsp garlic
1 tsp poppy seeds
¼ tsp turmeric powder
2 tsp chilli powder
Juice of 1 small lemon   B
¼ cup fresh curd
Salt to taste

For The Rice
1½ cups long grained rice
1 tsp garam masala
¼ tsp black cummin seeds
¼ tsp turmeric powder
2 tbsp hot melted ghee
24 fried cashewnut halves
1 tbsp raisins
½ tsp saffron dissolved in 1 tbsp hot milk
Salt to taste

METHOD

Grind together the items marked A and mix with items marked B, under marinade. Rub this mixture on the chicken pieces and set aside for 2 hours.

Pick, wash and soak the rice in water for about 15 minutes. Add salt and cook plain boiled rice in the usual manner, making sure that the rice is only half-cooked. Drain and cool at room temperature. Add garam masala, black cummin seeds, turmeric powder and ghee. Mix and set aside. Heat the oil and deep fry the onions till golden brown and crisp. Drain and set aside.

In a heavy-bottomed pan, heat 2 tablespoons oil and add the chicken along with the marinade, ¼ cup water and salt. Bring to a boil. Cook covered on a low flame for about 15 minutes, or until the chicken is slightly under-cooked. Add ½ the fried onions. Mix well and cover the chicken with the prepared rice. Sprinkle the remaining fried onions, cashewnuts, raisins and the saffron milk over the rice. Seal the pan with wheat flour dough and place the pan on a tawa over a low flame for about 15-20 minutes.

Remove the wheat flour dough just before serving. Serve the biryani very hot with Burhaani raita or vegetable raita.

SERVES : 4-6

Murg Masala
Spicy Chicken

A rich, spicy and flavoursome curry, usually served at parties, although it can also be used as a Sunday special. While frying the onions, it is very important to make them golden brown and crisp, as only then will it be possible to crush them easily. The main accompaniments to this are chappatis, parathas or naans.

INGREDIENTS

1 medium-sized chicken (approx 700 gms)
¼ cup water
2 cups chopped onion
2 cups oil
2 medium-sized Bay leaves
4 cloves
1½" piece cinnamon
2 cardamoms
10 cashewnuts
1½ tbsp poppy seeds
1 tbsp coriander powder
½ tsp turmeric powder
2 tsp chilli powder
1 tsp garam masala
Salt to taste

For The Marinade
1 green chilli
¾ cup corlander leaves
2 tbsp ginger
1½ tbsp garlic
½ tsp turmeric powder
1½ tsp chilli powder
Juice of 1 medium-sized lemon
½ cup fresh curd
Salt to taste

For Garnishing
8 almonds (blanch & cut each into 4 pieces
3 hard boiled eggs
(shell & cut each into 4 pieces)

METHOD

Cut the chicken into medium-sized pieces and wash well. Combine all the items mentioned under marinade. Rub this mixture on the chicken pieces and set aside for 2 hours.

Heat the oil and deep fry the onion till golden brown and crisp. Drain and place on a sieve to get rid of excess oil. When the onions become cold, crush and set aside,

Heat 2 tablespoons oil and add the Bay leaves, cloves, cinnamon and cardamoms and briefly fry. Add the ground cashewnuts, poppy seeds, coriander powder, turmeric powder, chilli powder, garam masala and salt. Stir and add the chicken along with the marinade, crushed onion and water. Bring to a boil and cook covered on a low flame for about 25 minutes or until the chicken is cooked. Stir 2-3 times in-between. Garnish with almonds and hard boiled eggs. Serve hot with tandoori rotis, naans or chappatis.

SERVES : 4-6

Shammi Kabab

Minced Meat and Lentil Kababs

A classic dish which is extremely popular as a starter, snack or as a side dish to a meal. The main accompaniments are coriander chutney or thin round slices of onion and small pieces of lemon.

INGREDIENTS

For The Filling
1 tbsp oil
1 small onion (peeled & chopped)
2 green chillies (chopped)
1 tsp poppy seeds
¼ tsp chilli powder
¼ tsp garam masala
1 tbsp raisins
1 tbsp tiny pieces of cashewnuts
Salt to taste

For The Kababs
500 gms minced meat
2 tbsp Bengal gram
1 large onion (peeled & chopped)
1 tbsp green chillies (chopped)
1 tsp ginger (chopped)
1 tsp garlic (chopped)
½ tsp turmeric powder
½ tsp chili powder
½ tsp garam masala
½ cup water
1 egg
Oil for frying
Salt for taste

Accompaniments
3 medium-sized onions (peeled & cut into thin rounds)
3 medium-sized lemons (cut into 4 pieces each)
Coriander chutney

METHOD

First prepare the filling. Heat the oil. Add the onion and green chillies. Fry for 2 minutes. Add the remaining ingredients and fry for 2 minutes. Remove from heat and set aside.

With the exception of the egg and oil, combine all the ingredients mentioned under Kababs. Pressure cook till done, (i.e. after 1 whistle, pressure cook on a low flame for about 2 minutes). When the pressure cooker is opened, cook uncovered on a high flame till the mixture becomes absolutely dry. Remove from heat and cool. Grind to a smooth mixture. Add the egg.

Divide the cooked minced meat mixture and the filling into equal portions. With moist hands, flatten a portion of the minced meat mixture on your palm, put a portion of the filling in the centre, enclose the filling completely and shape into a flat round kabab. Prepare the remaining kababs in the same manner. Place the prepared kababs in a covered container in the refrigerator for 30 minutes.

Heat the oil in a flat pan. Shallow fry the kababs, a few at a time. Drain when both sides become golden brown.

Serve hot with cocktails or as a snack at a party or as a side dish to a meal, accompanied by onion, lemon and coriander chutney.

SERVES : 4-6

Bhagarey Baigan
Spicy Curried Brinjals

Fried and spicy, this unusual preparation, in spite of using an ordinary vegetable like brinjal, tastes so delicious that it has become very famous and is often served on special occasions as well as holding a place on the weekly menu. Rub salt on the brinjals, set aside for 10 minutes and then squeeze out the salty water before flying them, as this removes the slight bitterness that is found in brinjals, besides allowing the salt to penetrate into them. The main accompaniments to this are chappatis or biryani.

INGREDIENTS

8 small brinjals
Oil for frying
20 curry leaves
1 tbsp ginger paste
1 tsp garlic paste
1 tsp turmeric powder
½ tsp chilli powder
6 green chillies (silt through the centre and kept whole)
¼ cup thick tamarind juice
1 cup water
Salt to taste

Roast In 1 tbsp Oil And Grind Together
¼ of a medium-sized dry coconut (grated)
1 tsp cummin seeds
1 tbsp coriander seeds
1 tbsp poppy seeds
1tbsp sesame seeds
2 tbsp peanuts without skin

METHOD

Cut each brinjal into fours, almost all the way, but keeping the base intact. Wash and rub salt all over and set aside for 10 minutes.

Heat the oil in a frying pan. When the oil becomes hot, squeeze out the water from the brinjals and deep fry them 4 at a time, carefully, making sure they do not break. Drain when light brown in colour. Set aside.

Heat 3 tablespoons of oil in a broad flat pan. Add the curry leaves, ginger and garlic. Stir quickly. Add the ground masala. Fry on a low flame for 3 minutes, stirring continuously. Add the turmeric powder, chilli powder and green chillies. Stir. Add the tamarind juice, water and salt. Bring to a boil. Reduce the flame and arrange the brinjals in a single layer in the gravy. Cook covered on a low flame for about 7 minutes, stirring twice in-between carefully, so that the brinjals do not break. Remove from heat. Serve hot with biryani or chappatis.

SERVES : 4-6

Burhaani Raita

Aromatic Curd Sauce

A good digestive and balancing accompaniment to a heavy biryani.
It has the predominant taste of garlic and a latent taste of mint. The
main accompaniment to this dish is a vegetarian or non-vegetarian biryani.

INGREDIENTS

3 cups thick fresh curd ⎤ Grind
6 cloves peeled garlic ⎬ to a
1 tbsp chopped mint leaves ⎦ paste
½ tsp pepper
Salt to taste

METHOD

Beat the curd without adding any water. When the curd becomes quite smooth, add the ground paste, pepper and salt. Beat this mixture until the curd becomes absolutely smooth. Chill on a refrigerator shelf.

Serve cold as an accompaniment to mutton, chicken or vegetable biryani.

SERVES : 4-6

Khubani Ka Meetha
Apricots with Custard

A highly nutritious dessert which contains milk and is therefore a good source of protein and calcium. Apricots are also a good source of iron. This preparation is extremely popular for weddings. An easy way to prepare apricot pulp, is to soak the apricots in cold water for about 8 hours and then rub them with your fingers.

INGREDIENTS

For The Apricot Pulp
22 dry apricots (khurmani or jardalu)
3¼ cups water
7 tbsp sugar
1 tbsp lemon juice

For The Custard
2 cups milk
2 ½ tbsp sugar
1½ tbsp custard powder mixed with
¼ cup cold milk

METHOD

Wash the apricots. Add 3 cups water. Bring to a boil. Cook covered on a low flame for about 10 minutes or until the apricots become very soft. Remove from heat and set aside until cold. Rub the apricots with your fingers in order to remove the seeds. Break the seeds and remove the almonds from them. Set aside the almonds. Reheat the apricot pulp, adding the sugar, lemon juice and ¼ cup water. Cook uncovered on a low flame for about 5 minutes or until the apricot pulp becomes thick, stirring often. Remove from heat and cool at room temperature. Then pour into a glass dish and chill on the refrigerator shelf.

Next prepare the custard. Bring the milk to a boil. Add the sugar and stir until the sugar melts. Add the custard powder mixed with ¼ cup cold milk. Stir continuously for 2 minutes, so that the milk becomes thick and smooth. Remove from heat and cool at room temperature.

Pour the custard on top of the chilled apricot pulp. Arrange the apricot and almonds on top of the custard. Chill once again on a refrigerator shelf.

Serve cold as a dessert.

SERVES : 4-6

Seviyon Ka Zarda
Vermicelli Delight

A rich and tasty delicacy generally served on the occasion of Id or on other days of celebration. Overcooking this dish should be avoided at any cost, as this spoils the appearance and taste totally. Overcooking makes the dish soggy, which is generally due to the addition of excess liquid while cooking

INGREDIENTS

4 tbsp melted ghee
2 crushed cardamoms
2 coarsely pounded cloves
100 gms (approx 2 cups) small pieces of roasted fine vermicelli
3 cups hot water
3/4 cup sugar
1 tbsp melted ghee (to be used at the end)

For Garnishing
1 tbsp blanched & chopped almonds
1 tbsp blanched & chopped pistachio nuts
¼ cup small pieces of solidified milk (mawa)
Silver leaf (optional)

METHOD

Heat 4 tablespoons ghee in a thick pan or a non-stick pan. Add the cardamoms and cloves briefly and fry for a minute. Add the vermicelli and fry on a low flame for 3 minutes, stirring continuously. Add the hot water and bring to a boil. Cover and cook on a low flame for about 5 minutes, stirring twice. Add the sugar and cook uncovered on a low flame, stirring carefully most of the time, for about 5 minutes or until the vermicelli is cooked and there is no moisture left. Add a teaspoon of ghee and stir.

Remove from heat and transfer the vermicelli into a serving bowl. Sprinkle the almonds, pistachio nuts and mawa on top. Cover with the silver leaf.

Serve hot as a sweet dish at any time. However, it can also be served as a dessert.

Note: In case unroasted vermicelli is used, fry for 5 minutes or until golden brown in colour, for which an additional 2 tablespoons of ghee will be required.

SERVES : 4-6

Sheer Khurma
Vermicelli Milk

A rich and luxurious concoction of milk, fried nuts and vermicelli, which is both superb and sustaining. This dish is generally served during Id and other special functions. If you want to serve hot Sheer Khurma, it is advisable to store the vermicelli milk and the fried dry fruits separately. At the time of serving, reheat the vermicelli milk, add the fried dry fruits and mix. This way, the crispy effect of the dry fruits will be retained.

INGREDIENTS

6 dry dates (soaked in a little water overnight)
1 tbsp raisins
1 tbsp medium-sized pieces of cashewnuts
1 tbsp charoli seeds (chironji)
1 tbsp medium-sized pieces of blanched almonds
1 tbsp medium-sized pieces of blanched pistachio nuts
2½ tbsp melted ghee
¼ cup roasted vermicelli (seviyan)
4 cups whole milk
2 crushed cardamoms
3½ tbsp sugar

METHOD

Remove the seeds from the dry dates and cut each date into 4 pieces. Combine the raisins, cashewnuts, charoli seeds, almonds and pistachio nuts. Heat the ghee and fry the mixed dry fruits on a low flame for about 2 minutes, stirring continuously. Drain and mix with the chopped dry dates. Set aside.

In the same ghee, fry the vermicelli on a low flame for about 2 minutes, stirring continuously. Removed from heat and set aside.

In a heavy pan, boil the milk and add the vermicelli, cardamoms and sugar. Stir until the sugar melts. Cook uncovered on a low flame for about 10 minutes, stirring often. Add the prepared dry fruits and cook for 3 minutes.

Serve hot or cold in individual bowls at any time. However, it can also be served as a dessert.

Note : In case unroasted vermicelli is used, fry a little longer to obtain a golden brown colour, for which an additional ½ tablespoon of ghee will be required.

SERVES : 4-6

Tamatar Chutney
Tomato Chutney

A delicious, aromatic side dish, quick and easy to prepare and very different from the usual chutneys. The main accompaniments to this dish are rice or vegetable pulao or parathas.

INGREDIENTS

4 tbsp oil
2 red chillies (whole)
½ tsp mustard seeds
½ tsp cummin seeds
½ tsp onion seeds
¼ tsp fenugreek seeds
6 large red tomatoes (immersed in hot water for
5 minutes, then drained, peeled & chopped)
2 tbsp vinegar
Salt to taste

Grind To A Paste With A Little Vinegar
1" piece ginger
6 cloves garlic
4 red chillies
1 tbsp coriander seeds
1 tsp cummin seeds
1 tsp poppy seeds

METHOD

Heat the oil. Add the red chillies, mustard seeds, cummin seeds, onion seeds and fenugreek seeds. When the mustard seeds splutter, add the ground paste and fry on a low flame for about 2 minutes, stirring continuously. Add the tomatoes. Cook covered on a low flame for about 5 minutes. Mash the tomatoes. Add the salt and vinegar. Cook uncovered on a low flame for 5 minutes, stirring often, so that the chutney does not stick to the bottom of the pan. When the chutney becomes quite thick, remove from heat.

Serve hot with rice, vegetable pulao or parathas.

SERVES : 4-6

Kashmiri

Dahi Gosht
Curd Mutton

Curd, an important ingredient in Kashmiri cuisine, enhances the taste of this dish, the preparation of which is quite simple and straightforward. The main accompaniment to this dish is rice chappatis or parathas.

INGREDIENTS

500 gms mutton
(cut into medium-sized pieces)
¹⁄₃ cup oil
A large pinch asafoetida mixed with 1 tsp water
4 cloves
1" stick cinnamon
3 cardamoms
1 tsp cummin seeds
1 tsp chilli powder
1 cup fresh curd (beaten)
1½ cups water
½ tsp turmeric powder
½ tsp dry ginger powder
¼ tsp garam masala
1 tbsp chopped mint leaves
Salt to taste

METHOD

Heat the oil. Add the asafoetida water and mutton. Fry on a medium flame for about 5 minutes, stirring often. Add the mixture of cloves, cinnamon, cardamoms and cummin seeds. Stir briefly. Add the chilli powder. Stir briefly. Add the curd. Cook uncovered on a medium flame for about 3 minutes, stirring often. Add the water, turmeric powder and salt.

Pressure cook the mutton till soft (i.e. after 1 whistle pressure cook on a low flame for about 15 minutes). When the pressure cooker is opened, add the ginger powder, garam masala and mint leaves. Stir. Cook uncovered on a low flame for 5 minutes. Serve hot with rice, chappatis or parathas.

SERVES : 4-6

Dum Bheja
Brain Curry

*Moderately spiced yet delicious, as well as quick and easy
to prepare. The main accompaniment to this
dish is rice or chappatis.*

INGREDIENTS

4 large goat's brains (bheja)
4 cups water

For The Gravy
2 tbsp oil
A pinch of asafoetida
3 cloves (coarsely crushed)
1 tbsp chopped ginger
½ cup fresh curd (beaten)
½ tsp chilli powder
1 tsp coriander powder
¼ tsp gram masala
1 cup water
Salt to taste

For Garnishing
¼ tsp garam masala
½ tsp dry ginger powder
3 tbsp chopped coriander leaves

METHOD

Wash the brains in plenty of water. Drain and discard impurities.

Heat the water. When it comes to a boil, add the brains and cook uncovered for 2 minutes. Remove from heat and keep covered for about 5 minutes. After 5 minutes, drain the brains from the water, cool and cut each into 6 pieces lengthwise. Set aside.

Next prepare the gravy. Heat the oil. Add the asafoetida, cloves and ginger. Stir. Add the curd, chilli powder, coriander powder and garam masala. Fry on a low flame for about 3 minutes, stirring continuously. Add the water, brain pieces and salt. Bring to a boil. Cook covered on a low flame for about 7 minutes, stirring twice in-between. Garnish with the garam masala, ginger powder and coriander leaves. Serve hot with chappatis or rice.

SERVES : 4-6

Kalai

Stewed Yellow Meat

This easy-to-prepare dish, despite being low in fat and spices, is aromatic and tastes delicious. The main accompaniment to this dish is rice.

INGREDIENTS

500 gms mutton (raan i.e. hind leg)
4 tbsp oil
A pinch asafoetida mixed with 1 tsp water
1 tsp cummin seeds
1 tsp aniseeds } Grind
4 cloves } to a
2 black cardamoms } powder
½ tsp chilli powder
½ tsp sugar
¾ tsp turmeric powder
1½ cups water
½ tsp dry ginger powder
Salt to taste

METHOD

Cut the mutton into medium-sized pieces. Wash and set aside.

Heat the oil. Add the asafoetida water. Then add the mutton, powdered cummin seeds, aniseeds, cloves, cardamoms, chilli powder, sugar and salt. Fry on a medium flame for about 5 minutes, stirring most of the time. Add the turmeric powder. Stir. Add the water. Pressure cook till done (i.e. after 1 whistle, pressure cook on a low flame about 12 minutes).

When the pressure cooker is opened, add the dry ginger powder. Cook covered on a low flame for 3 minutes. Serve hot with rice.

SERVES : 4-6

Roghan Josh
Rich Mutton Curry

A classic dish prepared in the traditional Kashmiri style, it is one of the best and most famous meat dishes–simply marvellous in appearance, aroma and taste. This dish is generally served at weddings and on days of celebration. The main accompaniments to this dish are fulkas, tandoori rotis, naans, or chappatis.

INGREDIENTS

500 gms mutton (front leg)
4 tbsp oil
4 cloves
½" piece cinnamon
2 cardamoms
A pinch of asafoetida
3 tsp chilli powder (bright red variety)
1 tsp dry aniseed powder (sonth)
1 tsp aniseed powder
1 cup beaten curd
1 cup water
½ tsp sugar (optional)
¼ cup mawa mixed with ¼ cup beaten curd
10 almonds (ground to a paste)
1 tsp garam masala
Salt to taste

METHOD

Cut the mutton into 1½" pieces and wash. Drain and set aside.

Heat the oil and add the cloves, cinnamon, cardamom and asafoetida. Stir and add the mutton pieces. Fry uncovered over a medium flame for about 5 minutes, stirring often. Add 2 teaspoons chilli powder, the dry ginger powder, aniseed powder, salt and curd. Cook covered on a low flame, stirring twice or thrice till the liquid dries up and the masala sticks to the bottom of the pan. Scrape the scorched masala from the bottom of the pan. Add ¼ cup water and cook covered till the masala sticks to the bottom of the pan. Add the remaining ¾ cup water and sugar. Pressure cook till the mutton becomes soft (i.e. after one whistle, pressure cook on a low flame for about 10 minutes). When the pressure cooker is opened, add the mawa-curd mixture, ground almonds, garam masala and the remaining teaspoon of chilli powder. Cook uncovered on a low flame for about 5 minutes. Stir once. Serve hot with tandoori rotis, naans or chappatis.

SERVES : 4-6

Badam Pista Firni
Nutty Milk Pudding

A mere glimpse of this pudding, particularly in earthen bowls,
topped with a variety of nuts, is enough to make it unforgettable.
Moreover, it is so simple and quick to prepare.

INGREDIENTS

12 almonds
(blanched & ground to a paste with ½ cup milk)
4 tbsp rice flour
2 ½ cups milk
5 tbsp sugar
8 strands saffron
4 crushed cardamoms

For Garnishing
8 almonds
8 pistachio nuts
Silver leaf (optional)

Blauched and chopped into thin long pieces

METHOD

Combine the ground almonds and rice flour. Mix well and set aside.

Bring the milk to a boil. Add the sugar. Stir till the sugar dissolves. Remove a tablespoon of hot milk and add the saffron to it. Rub the saffron strands with your fingers. When the saffron is well dissolved, add the saffron milk to the boiling milk. Then add the almond and rice flour mixture. Stir continuously for a few minutes till the milk looks like a custard. Sprinkle in the crushed cardamoms. Remove from heat. Cool at room temperature.

Divide the firni between 4 or 6 individual dessert bowls. If earthen bowls are available, use these so that the firni acquires an extraordinary flavour. Arrange the chopped almonds and pistachio nuts and the silver leaf on top of the firni. Then chill in the refrigetor.

Serve cold as a dessert.

SERVES : 4-6

Bhasbhatta
Special Pulao

An unusual aromatic and spicy pulao for vegetarians, most suitable for a Sunday lunch. The best part is that it is quick and simple to prepare. The main accompaniment to this dish is potato raita, plain curd or pickle.

INGREDIENTS

1½ cups long-grained rice
½ cup chana dal
4 tbsp oil
A pinch of asafoetida
¼ tsp cummin seeds
4 cloves
2 cardamoms
3 small sticks cinnamon
8 peppercorns
2 small Bay leaves
1 cup long thin onion pieces
1 tbsp chopped ginger
1½ tsp chilli powder
½ tsp turmeric powder
½ tsp garam masala
3 medium potatoes (peeled & halved)
3 cups water
¼ cup chopped coriander leaves
Salt to taste

METHOS

Pick, wash and soak the rice and chana dal in water, separately, for about 30 minutes.

Heat the oil and then add the asafoetida, cummin seeds, cloves, cardamoms, cinnamon, peppercorns and Bay leaves. Stir quickly and add the onion, ginger and the drained chana dal. Fry uncovered on a low flame for about 5 minutes, stirring continuously. Add the chilli powder, turmeric powder, garam masala and potatoes. Fry in the same manner for about 3 minutes, stirring continuously. Add the drained rice, water and salt. Pressure cook the Bhasbhatta until tender but not overcooked (i.e. after one whistle, pressure cook on a low flame for about 5 minutes).

Garnish with coriander leaves and serve piping hot with potato raita, plain curd or pickle.

SERVES : 4-6

Dum Aloo
Potato Curry

Fried potatoes are cooked in a rich gravy in the traditional Kashmiri style. This is one of the best potato dishes, generally served at parties, although it is popular for everyday meals too. Always ensure that the potatoes are pricked before frying because this will enable the gravy to penetrate into the potatoes, making them more tasty. The main accompaniments to this dish are fulkas, tandoori rotis, naans, parathas or chappatis.

INGREDIENTS

10 medium-sized potatoes
A pinch of asafoetida
½ tsp cummin seeds
2 cloves
2 cardamoms
2 small sticks cinnamon
1 medium-sized onion (peeled)
2 green chillies   } Grind to a paste
2 medium-sized tomatoes
1" piece ginger
2 Kashmiri red chillies
(soaked in ¼ cup hot water for 15 minutes)
1 cup fresh curd (beaten)
¾ tsp turmeric powder
½ tsp chilli powder
1½ cups water
½ tsp garam masala
¼ tsp dry ginger powder
¼ cup chopped coriander leaves
Oil for frying
Salt to taste

METHOD

Boil the potatoes in a pressure cooker. Cool and peel. Prick the surface of the potatoes with a fork, toothpick or knitting needle. Heat the oil and deep fry the potatoes in two batches. Drain when uniformly brown. Set aside.

In a separate pan, heat 2 tablespoons oil. Now add the asafoetida, cummin seeds, cloves, cardamoms and cinnamon. Stir quickly and add the ground paste. Fry the ground paste on a low flame for about 7 minutes, stirring frequently. Add the beaten curd, turmeric powder and chilli powder. Stir well and add the water, salt and the fried potatoes. Bring to a boil. Cook covered on a low flame for about 7 minutes, stirring twice or thrice. Add the garam masala and dry ginger powder. Stir. Garnish with coriander leaves and serve hot with tandoori rotis, naans, parathas or chappatis.

SERVES : 4-6

Fulka
Unleavened Bread

These puffed chappatis are not only satisfying but are also a visual delight. Served without ghee, they are absolutely low fat, although the application of a little ghee makes them irresistible. They are best served as soon as they are prepared. Therefore, it is necessary for one person to be free to prepare the fulkas and serve them in this manner to the others. The main accompaniment to this dish is any vegetable or meat preparation with or without gravy.

INGREDENTS

2 cups wheat flour
Water
1 tsp oil
A little melted ghee

METHOD

Add water, little by little, to the flour and prepare a dough similar to that for chappatis. Set aside, duly covered, for 15 minutes. Add a teaspoon of oil and knead the dough once again so as to make it absolutely smooth. Divide the dough into 12 portions.

Make a ball from each portion, flatten it a bit between the palms, making sure the edges are smooth. Dip each flattened ball in dry flour and roll out into a thin chappati, making sure the edges are not cracked. Heat a griddle (i.e. tawa) and wipe it very well after putting a few drops of oil on it. After wiping, there should be no trace of oil on it. Put one rolled chappati on the tawa and when the underside is done, turn over and allow the other side to be cooked lightly. Then lift with the help of tongs and place the top portion on the open flame of a gas burner. When it puffs up, turn over and slightly cook the other side on the flame, so that it becomes somewhat crisp. Remove from the fire and apply a little ghee on one side only if desired. Prepare the remaining fulkas in the same manner.

Serve hot with any vegetable or meat preparation.

SERVES : 4-6

Lauki Yakhni
Bottle Gourd Stew

So easy to prepare and yet so delicious that the taste lingers.
The incorporation of curd works wonders. Do not make
the mistake of reducing the quantity of curd, as this can
make or mar this dish. The main accompaniment
to this dish is rice, chappatis or parathas.

INGREDIENTS

600 gms long thin bottle gourd
Oil for frying
A big pinch of asafoetida mixed with 1 tsp water
2 tsp aniseed powder
3 tsp coriander powder
½ tsp dry ginger powder
2 green chillies (each cut into 4 pieces)
3¾ cup water
3 cups curd (beaten)
3 cloves
1" stick cinnamon
2 black cardamoms   Coarsely
2 cardamoms   crushed
½ tsp cummin seeds   and
Salt to taste   mixed
                        together

METHOD

Peel the bottle gourd and cut into ½" thick round pieces. Keep the small rounds whole and cut the bigger rounds into 2 pieces each, through the centre. Wash and wipe dry with a clean napkin.

Heat the oil in a pan. Deep fry the bottle gourd pieces. Drain when light brown in colour. Set aside.

Heat 2 tablespoons oil in a separate pan. Add the asafoetida water, aniseed powder, coriander powder, ginger powder and green chillies. Stir quickly. Add the fried bottle gourd, water and salt. Cook covered on a low flame for about 3 minutes. Add the curd and mixture of cloves, cinnamon, cardamoms and cummin seeds gradually, stirring continuously.

Cook uncovered on a low flame for about 5 minutes or until the bottle gourd is soft.

Serve hot with rice, chappatis or parathas.

SERVES : 4-6

Methi Chaman

Cottage Cheese with Fenugreek

A simple method is used to prepare this nutritious, aromatic and popular dish, which can be served on special occasions as well as on ordinary days. While frying the paneer, always ensure that the frying is very light, as too much frying will make the paneer hard, which is undesirable. The main accompaniments to this dish are fulkas, chappatis or rice.

INGREDIENTS

Oil for frying
30 pieces chaman (paneer) size 1" x ½"
1 tbsp oil
A pinch of asafoetida
½ tsp cummin seeds
2 cups fresh methi leaves or
2 cups dry methi (kasoori methi)
1 tsp green chillies (chopped)
1 tsp chopped ginger
1 tbsp powdered almonds
½ tsp turmeric powder
½ tsp chilli powder
1 tsp coriander powder
½ cup fresh curd (beaten)
1½ cups water
¼ tsp gram masala
¼ tsp dry ginger powder
1 tbsp grated ginger
Salt to taste

METHOD

Heat the oil. Fry the paneer pieces a few at a time. Drain when light brown in colour and soak in ½ cup of water. Set aside.

Heat a tablespoon of oil. Add the asafoetida and cummin seeds. Stir. Add the ground paste and powdered almonds. Fry on a low flame for 3 minutes, stirring often. Add the turmeric powder, chilli powder, coriander powder and curd. Stir for 2 minutes. Add the remaining cup of water as well as the salt. Bring to a boil. Cook uncovered on a low flame for about 5 minutes. Add the fried paneer pieces together with the water in which they were soaked. Cook uncovered on a medium flame for about 5 minutes, stirring twice carefully, so that the paneer pieces do not break. Remove from heat.

Garnish with garam masala, ginger powder and grated ginger. Serve hot with chappatis or rice.

SERVES : 4-6

Nadru Pakora
Lotus Stem Fries

A delicacy indeed. It is often selected as a tasty cocktail snack.
The main accompaniment to this dish is coriander chutney.

INGREDIENTS

12 pieces of lotus stem (kamal kakri) 3" long
¼ tsp soda bi carbonate
Oil for frying
Salt to taste

For The Batter
1½ cups gram flour
A pinch of soda bi carbonate
$1/8$ tsp orange-red food colouring
½ tsp thymol seeds (ajwain)
1 tsp cummin seeds (coarsely crushed)
2 tsp chilli powder
1 cup fresh curd (beaten)
A little water
Salt to taste

METHOD

Scrape the lotus stems and cut each into 2 pieces through the centre. Wash thoroughly in order to discard all the mud. Flatten each piece carefully with a mallet or grinding stone, when each piece may break into 2 pieces. Apply soda bi carbonate and salt on all the pieces. Set aside.

Combine all the ingredients mentioned under Batter and prepare a batter of medium consistency. Heat the oil in a frying pan. Dip each piece of lotus stem in the prepared batter and deep fry on a low flame. Drain when the pakoras become crisp and brown, by which time the lotus stem will also become tender. If the pakoras stick to one another, separate them with your fingers.

Serve hot with cocktails or as a snack, accompanied by coriander chutney.

SERVES : 4-6

Pudina Burhaani

Curd Sauce with Mint

An aromatic and slightly hot accompaniment to a meal.
It is low on fat, nutritious and the easiest thing to prepare.

INGREDIENTS

2½ cups fresh curd
Salt to taste

For The Masala Paste
1 cup fresh or dry mint leaves
3 medium-sized fresh red chillies
(green chillies turned red)
¼ cup water
Salt to taste

METHOD

Combine all the ingredients mentioned under Masala Paste. Grind to a very fine paste and set aside.

Add a little salt to the curd and beat till it becomes smooth. Add the ground paste and beat once again, so that everything is well mixed. Chill on a refrigerator shelf.

Serve as an accompaniment to a meal.

SERVES : 4-6

Shufta
Dry Fruit Delight

A rich accompaniment to a meal, comprising of a host of dry fruits, paneer, coconut and so on. It is considered a delicacy and used mainly during parties as an equaliser (i.e. to balance the burning sensation in the mouth when a number of spicy dishes are served). Unlike other dishes, serve merely a tablespoon of Shufta to each person along with the meal, as this is not a dessert, but only an equaliser, although one is surely tempted to take a bigger helping, as the dish is so tasty.

INGREDIENTS

½ cup small pieces of mixed dry fruits
(dry dates, figs, apricots, almonds,
pistachio nuts, raisins, walnuts)
Ghee for frying
1 tbsp small pieces of dry coconut
¼ cup cottage cheese (paneer) size ¼" x ¼"

For The Syrup
¼ cup sugar
¼ cup water
½ tsp milk
4 strands saffron (mixed in 1 tsp hot water)

METHOD

Before chopping the dry fruits, boil all the fruits, except the walnuts, in a small quantity of water. Drain and cool. Remove the seeds from the dry dates and the peels from the almonds and pistachio nuts. Then chop all the fruits into small pieces. Set aside.

Heat the ghee. Deep fry all the dry fruits and coconut together. Drain. In the same ghee, deep fry the paneer. Drain when light brown in colour. Combine the fried dry fruits, coconut and paneer. Set aside.

Next prepare the syrup. Combine the sugar, water and milk. Stir till the sugar melts. Remove from heat and strain. Reheat the syrup. Add the saffron and the fried dry fruit, coconut and paneer mixture. Cook uncovered on a low flame for a few minutes until the mixture becomes quite dry but not completely so.

Serve at room temperature. Each person can eat a tablespoon or so of Shufta, a little at a time during the meal, to balance spicy food.

SERVES : 4-6

Maharashtrian

Bhoojan

Pomfret with Onion and Garlic

*The onions and garlic which dominate this dish give it a
delicious taste which is sure to linger. Moreover, it is quick
and easy to prepare. The main accompaniment
to this dish is rice or chappatis.*

INGREDIENTS

2 medium-sized pomfrets
(cut into 6 pieces each)
6 tbsp oil
5 medium-sized onions (peeled & chopped)
½" piece ginger (scraped & chopped)
15 cloves garlic (peeled & chopped)
5 green chillies (chopped)
½ cup water
½ tsp turmeric powder
1 tsp chilli powder
6 cocums
½ cup grated coconut
¼ cup chopped coriander leaves
Salt to taste

METHOD

Wash the pomfret pieces and drain. Heat the oil. Add the onions and fry till transparent but not brown. Add the ginger, garlic and green chillies. Fry for a minute. Add the pomfret water and the remaining ingredients. Bring to a boil. Cover with a lid. Put a little water on the lid. Cook on a low flame for about 7 minutes, stirring once in-between very carefully so that the pieces of pomfret do not break.

Serve hot with rice or chappatis.

SERVES : 4-6

Masaledar Andi
Spicy Eggs

*An **economical** dish which can be prepared on the spur of the moment as eggs are generally very handy. After placing the eggs in the gravy, stir them very carefully, so that they do not break, as whole eggs have their own charm. The main accompaniment to this dish is chappatis or rice.*

INGREDIENTS

2 tbsp oil
2 medium-sized onions (peeled & chopped)
1 tbsp ginger paste
1 tsp garlic paste
½ tsp turmeric powder
1¼ cups water
2 tbsp thick tamarind juice
6 hardboiled eggs
2 tbsp chopped coriander leaves
Salt to taste

For The Masala Paste
2 tbsp oil
1 medium-sized onion (peeled & chopped)
½ cup grated coconut
2 cloves
1 Bay leaf
6 peppercorns
6 red chillies
½" stick cinnamon
1 tsp coriander seeds
1 tsp poppy seeds

METHOD

First prepare the Masala paste. Heat the oil and fry the onion and coconut separately until brown. Set aside. In the same oil fry the remaining ingredients for 30 seconds. Combine the onion, coconut and the rest of the ingredients and grind to a smooth paste. Set aside.

Next prepare the gravy. Heat the oil. Add the onion and fry until light brown in colour. Add the ground paste, ginger and garlic and fry for 2 minutes. Add the turmeric powder, water, salt and tamarind juice. Bring to a boil. Cook uncovered on a low flame for about 5 minutes.

Shell the eggs and cut each into quarters, keeping the base intact. Put the eggs into the gravy. Cook uncovered on a low flame for about 5 minutes. Garnish with coriander leaves. Serve hot with chappatis or rice.

SERVES : 4-6

Matnachi Curry
Mutton Curry

*Coconut and onion fried and ground with other spices, are
incorporated in this curry prepared in the traditional
Maharashtrian style. The result – a unique flavour. The main
accompaniment to this dish is chappatis or rice.*

INGREDIENTS

500 gms mutton
¾ tsp turmeric powder
1 tsp chilli powder
1 tsp garam masala
2½ cups water
Salt to taste

Masala (A)
5 cloves garlic
½" piece ginger   Grind
4 green chillies   to a
1 cup coriander leave ⌋ paste

Masala (B)   Fry
1 cup scraped cocount coconut &
3 medium onions   onions in
2 tbsp oil   the oil,
                       then grind
                       to a paste

For The Vaghar
3 tbsp oil
5 cloves garlic (peeled & kept whole)
2 tbsp chopped onion

METHOD

Clean and wash the mutton after cutting into
medium-sized pieces. Rub Masala (A) on the
mutton pieces and set aside for about 15 minutes.

Heat the oil and add the garlic and onion
(mentioned under vaghar). Fry for a minute. Add
the masala-coated mutton pieces and fry over a
medium flame for about 10 minutes, stirring often.
Add the turmeric powder, chilli powder, garam
masala, salt and water.

Pressure cook the mutton till it becomes tender
(i.e. after 1 whistle, pressure cook on a low flame
for about 15 minutes). When the pressure cooker
is opened add Masala (B) and cook uncovered
on a low flame for about 7 minutes, stirring twice
or thrice. Serve hot with rice or chappatis.

SERVES : 4-6

Paplet Thapthapit
Pomfret in Green Masala

*The ground green masala, together with the whole garlic,
makes this dish superb. The main accompaniment to
it is chappatis or rice.*

INGREDIENTS

1 medium-sized pomfret (cut into 6 pieces)
½ of a fresh coconut
½ cup coriander leaves   } Grind to a paste
5 cloves garlic
2 tbsp oil
2 tbsp chopped onion
4 cloves garlic (peeled & kept whole)
1½ cups water
½ tsp turmeric powder
2 tsp chilli powder
8 black cocums
Salt to taste

METHOD

Wash the pomfret pieces well in water and then drain. Rub the ground paste on the pomfret pieces and set aside for 5 minutes.

Heat the oil and add the onion. Fry on a low flame for about 3 minutes. Add the whole garlic flakes and fry for a minute. Add the masala-coated pomfret pieces along with the water, turmeric powder, chilli powder, salt and the cocums. Bring to a boil, reduce flame and cook partly covered for about 7 minutes, stirring once or twice very carefully, so that the pomfret pieces do not break.

Serve hot with rice or chappatis.

SERVES : 4-6

Sookhi Kolmi

Dry Prawns

*A quick and easy way to prepare prawns on a tawa. The result –
a fresh and unusual taste. Since the prawns are prepared on a griddle
(tawa), reheating should also be done on a tawa, as this lends a special
flavour to the dish. The main accompaniments are puris or chappatis.*

INGREDIENTS

2 cups shelled and deveined prawns
2 tbsp oil
5 cloves garlic (peeled & kept whole)
2 medium-sized onions (peeled & chopped)
½ tsp turmeric powder
2 tsp chilli powder
¾ tsp garam masala
6 cocums
¾ cup water
2 tbsp chopped coriander leaves
Salt to taste

METHOD

Heat the oil on a tawa and add the garlic cloves. Fry for a minute. Add the onion and fry on a low flame, stirring often. When the onion becomes brown in colour, add the turmeric powder and chilli powder. Stir quickly and add the prawns, garam masala, salt, cocums and water. Bring to a boil. Reduce flame and cook uncovered for about 10 minutes, stirring often. Add the coriander leaves when the prawns become almost dry.

Serve hot with puris or chappatis.

SERVES : 4-6

Basundi

Thickened Milk

A rich and nutritious dessert – a favourite with young and old alike.
It can be served hot or cold in any season. Cold Basundi is often
served at weddings. The main accompaniment to this dish is puris.

INGREDIENTS

6 cups milk
6 tbsp sugar
1 tbsp raisins (optional)
½ tsp cardamom powder
¹/₃ tsp nutmeg powder

For Garnishing
6 almonds (blanched & cut into
long thin pieces)
8 pistachio nuts (blanched and cut into
long thin pieces)
1 tbsp charoli

METHOD

Boil the milk in a thick-bottomed pan. Stir continuously on a high flame, making sure the milk does not spill over. Do not keep the flame low as this will change the colour of the basundi to off-white. The ideal colour of basundi is white, although there is nothing wrong in making an off-white coloured basundi, in which case, the milk may be thick ened on a low flame. When the milk is reduced to almost half, add the sugar and raisins. Stir till the sugar dissolves. Add the cardamom and nutmeg powders. Stir and remove from heat. Pour the contents into a serving dish. Garnish with almonds, pistachio nuts and charoli.

Serve piping hot or cold with puris. For cold basundi, chill in the refrigerator. Basundi can also be served as a dessert.

Variation : For weddings and special occasions, make an exotic dish called *Angoor Basundi*. Simmer the milk for about 20 minutes, add 24 angoor (tiny) rasgullas, making sure they are below the milk level and cook uncovered on a medium flame for about 5 minutes. It is, however, very important to note that a negligible amount of sugar should be used, as the rasgullas are already sweet.

SERVES : 4-6

Bharleli Wangi
Stuffed Brinjals

The peanuts and coconut make this dish most nutritious, delicious and satisfying. The main accompaniments to this dish are chappatis.

INGREDIENTS

8 small brinjals
4 small potatoes
4 tbsp oil
2 medium-sized onions
(peeled & chopped)
¼ cup coarsely ground peanuts witnout skin
Salt to taste

For The Stuffing
½ cup grated coconut
¼ cup chopped coriander leaves
1 tbsp gram flour
½ tsp turmeric powder
1 tsp chIlli powder
½ tsp garam masala
1 tbsp oil
Salt to taste

⎫
⎬ Mix
⎭ together

METHOD

Trim the brinjals and peel the potatoes. Wash both. Cut the brinjals and potatoes into fours, almost all the way, keeping the base intact.

Stuff the brinjals and potatoes with the stuffing mixture. Set aside.

Heat the oil in a broad pan. Add the onions. Fry on a low flame for about 5 minutes or until the onions become light brown in colour. Add the peanuts and salt and fry for 2 minutes. Arrange the stuffed brinjals and potatoes on the onion-peanut mixture in a single layer. Cover the pan. Pour ½ cup water on the lid. Cook on a low flame for about 20 minutes or until the vegetables are ready. Stir very carefully 4 times in-between, pouring a little water from the lid onto the vegetables each time. Serve hot with chappatis.

SERVES : 4-6

Cocum Saar
Cocum Extract

An attractive drink with digestive properties, served as the last course of a heavy meal. The best part is that it is quick, economical and easy to make, as no cooking is required. The main accompaniment to this preparation is rice.

INGREDIENTS

6 black cocums
$1/3$ cup water
1 medium -sized coconut (grated)
1 green chilli
1 clove garlic
2 cups water
2 tbsp chopped coriander leaves
Salt to taste

METHOD

Wash the cocums. Soak them in water for about 10 minutes.

Blend the coconut, green chilli, garlic and water in a mixer. Remove from the mixer and pass through a sieve.

Add the coconut milk to the cocums, together with the water in which the cocums were soaked. Add salt and the coriander leaves. Serve cold or at room temperature. However, if serving is delayed for many hours, store in the refrigerator and remove it about 30 minutes before serving.

Have the cocum saar with a small quantity of rice as a last course. Cocum saar can also be drunk during a meal. The cocums should be squeezed and discarded while eating.

SERVES : 4-6

Kanda Bhajjia
Onion Fries

A quick and easy snack which can be prepared at short notice, as both onions and gram flour, the two main ingredients required for this dish, are generally handy. After the bhajjias have been fried, do not cover them, as the crispiness will be lost. Should covering become necessary, use a wire mesh dome instead. The main accompaniment to this dish is dry garlic-red chilli chutney or green cocount chutney.

INGREDIENTS

3 cups long thin slices of onion
3 cups gram flour (besan)
2 green chillies (chopped)
4 tbsp chopped coriander leaves
1½ tbsp coriander seeds (optional)
6 tbsp water
Oil for frying
Salt to taste

METHOD

Combine the onion, gram flour, green chillies, coriander leaves, salt and coriander seeds. Add water, little by little, and prepare a thick mixture. Set aside.

Heat the oil in a frying pan. When the oil smokes, remove 1 teaspoon of this oil and add it to the prepared bhajjia mixture and then beat well. Make 24 portions from this mixture and drop 8 portions at a time, one by one lengthwise, into the oil, making sure they do not stick to one another. Drain when golden brown all over.

Serve hot as a snack or a side dish to a meal, accompanied by dry garlic-red chilli chutney or green coconut chutney.

SERVES : 4-6

Masala Bhaat
Spicy Pulao

A very special pulao with a magnificent blend of spices and vegetables.
This pulao is generally served at Maharashtrian weddings.

INGREDIENTS

1½ cups short-grained rice
4 tbsp oil
A pinch of asafoetida
¾ tsp mustard seeds
4 medium-sized slit green chillies
¾ tsp turmeric powder
10 medium-sized gherkins(tendli),
each cut into 4 pieces lengthwise
½ cup green peas (shelled)
½ tsp coriander seeds ⎤ Roast in
½ tsp cummin seeds ⎟ a pan
1" piece cinnamon ⎬ without
¼ tsp black cummin seeds ⎟ oil and
1 tsp sesame seeds ⎦ grind to a
powder
1½ tsp garam masala
1½ tsp chilli powder
3 cups water
1 tsp lemon juice
1½ tsp small pieces cashewnuts
1½ tbsp raisins
1½ tbsp small pieces fresh cocount
Salt to taste

METHOD

Pick, wash and soak the rice in water for 10 minutes. Drain the rice and set aside, so that it becomes slightly dry.

Heat the oil in a pan and add the asafoetida and mustard seeds. When the mustard seeds splutter, add the green chillies and turmeric powder. Stir quickly and add the gherkins and green peas. Cook covered on a low flame for about 3 minutes, stirring twice. Add the rice and fry over a medium flame for about 5 minutes, stirring often. Add the ground masala powder, garam masala and chilli powder. Stir quickly and add the water, lemon juice and salt. Bring to a boil. Reduce flame to low and cook covered for about 15 minutes, stirring a few times very carefully, so that the rice does not get mashed.

When the rice is cooked, arrange the cashewnuts, raisins and coconut pieces on top of the rice in a decorative manner. Serve hot.

SERVES : 4-6

Missal
Spicy Mixture

A highly nutritious, economical, tasty, quick and easy snack.
If this dish is chosen for a party, serve the cooked white peas and
the accompaniments in separate bowls, but keep them together
in a broad tray, so that it is convenient to do the mixing to suit
individual tastes. This way, the Missal will not become soggy.

INGREDIENTS

1½ cups dry white peas (watana)
½ tsp turmeric powder
2 tbsp thick tamarind juice
1½ tbsp oil
½ tsp mustard seeds
1 tbsp chopped ginger
1 tsp chopped garlic
2 green chillies (chopped)
½ tsp garam masala
¼ tsp garam masala
¼ cup chopped coriander leaves
Salt to taste

Accompaniments
2 cups mixture of gathia, papri,
bhavnagri, peanuts, dal, etc.
¾ cup chopped onion
2 green chopped chillies
2 tbsp chopped coriander leaves
1 cup salty fresh curd, beaten

METHOD

Pick, wash and soak the peas in water overnight or for at least 8 hours. Add the turmeric powder and salt and pressure cook with very little water until the peas turn soft but are not overcooked. When the pressure cooker is opened, retain only ½ cup water and discard the rest. Add the tamarind juice. Set aside.

Heat the oil in a pan. Add the mustard seeds. When they splutter, add the ground paste. Fry for a minute and add to the cooked peas. Bring to a boil. Cook uncovered on a low flame for 2 minutes. Add the chilli powder, garam masala and coriander leaves. Mix well and remove from heat.

At the time of serving, pour the hot peas into individual serving dishes. Sprinkle the mixture of gathia, papri, etc, followed by the onion, green chillies and coriander leaves all over the cooked peas. Finally, top with a little curd in the centre. Serve immediately so that the gathia mixture does not turn soggy.

SERVES : 4-6

Pav Bhaji

Bread with Vegetables

An evergreen dish which is not only delicious but also nutritious and easy to prepare. Above all, it can be served at any time and even on special occasions. The aroma and superb taste of Pav Bhaji prepared on a tawa is sure to linger.

INGREDIENTS

8 small bread buns (paav) or
16 thick slices from loaf bread
1 *very* small head of cauliflower (approx 100 gms)
8 medium-sized potatoes (boiled, peeled & cubed)
3 large tomatoes (chopped)
1 medium-sized capsicum
(deseeded & cut into small pieces)
1 cup chopped onion
4 green chillies ⎫
½" piece ginger ⎬ Grind to a paste
10 cloves ⎭
1 tsp chilli powder
1 tsp garam masala
¼ cup chopped coriander leaves
¾ cup oil
1 cup butter
Salt to taste

METHOD

Cut the cauliflower into 4 pieces, trim the base and wash in plenty of water. Wipe with a clean napkin. Heat the oil in a pan and fry the cauliflower pieces. Drain when light brown in colour and set aside. In the same oil, add 2 tablespoons butter and the onion. Fry the onion on a low flame until it becomes transparent. Add the ground paste and fry for 3 minutes. Add the capsicum and tomatoes and cook uncovered for a minute on a low flame. Add the cauliflower, potatoes, turmeric powder, chilli powder, garam masala and salt. Mash roughly with a flat spatula on a low flame. Simmer uncovered for about 3 minutes, stirring twice. Garnish with coriander leaves. This is the Bhaji.

Next prepare the Pavs. If you are using small bread buns, cut each into 2 pieces through the centre. Melt a little butter on a tawa and place a piece of bread on it. Turn it quickly, so that the other side also gets coated with butter. Add more butter as required. In the same manner, fry all the remaining pavs.

Place the buttered pavs on a serving dish and the bhaji in another. Serve very hot without delay. The pavs should be eaten with the bhaji.

Pav Bhaji can be served as a snack or a meal-in-a-dish. The bhaji will have a special taste if prepared on a thick flat tawa. If softer bread pieces are preferred, additional butter can be used in the preparation.

SERVES : 4-6

Ragda-Pattis
White Peas and Potato Cakes

An extremely popular and famous two-in-one dish. It is a hot favourite with both children and adults and is an ideal choice for birthday and other parties. Ragda Pattis can also be served as two separate snacks. If ragda is served by itself, it becomes a low fat dish, as not a drop of oil is used in this method. The main accompaniments to this dish are green chilli chutney, sweet chutney and finely chopped onion.

INGREDIENTS

For The Ragda
2 cups dry white peas
½ tsp turmeric powder
1 tsp mango powder
1 tsp garam masala
2 tbsp chopped coriander leaves

For The Pattis
4 large potatoes
2 slices bread
Oil for frying
Salt to taste

For The Accompaniments
2 tbsp roasted cummin powder
2 tbsp chilli powder
½ cup green chilli chutney
1 cup sweet chutney
1cup chopped onion

METHOD

Pick, wash and soak the gram in water either overnight or for a minimum of 8 hours. Next morning, add the turmeric powder and salt.

Pressure cook the gram until soft, making sure it is not overcooked and mashed. Check the consistency, adding more water if necessary. Add the mango powder and garam masala. Cook on a low flame for about 5 minutes. Add the coriander leaves. Set aside.

Now prepare the pattis. Boil, peel and mash the potatoes, so that there are absolutely no lumps. Soak the bread in water, and squeeze. Mix the potatoes, bread pulp and salt. Make ¼" thin pattis, having a diametre of about 1½" . Heat a little oil on a tawa or flat non-stick pan and shallow fry the pattis, until crisp and golden brown on both sides.

Serve the hot pattis along with hot ragda placed side by side on the same plate. Add the chutney and sprinkle the cummin powder, chilli powder and onion on top of the ragda to suit individual tastes.

Ragda and pattis can also be served separately along with the accompaniments.

Serve this dish as a snack, quick-bite or at birthday parties, accompanied by green chilli chutney and sweet chutney and finely chopped onions.

SERVES : 4-6

Tomatao Saar
Tomato Extract

*When tomatoes are in season, it would make sense to choose
this nutritious and tasy dish as an accompaniment to rice,
in place of the usual dal.*

INGREDIENTS

6 medium-sized red juicy tomatoes
1½ cups water
2 tbsp grated coconut
2 green chillies (chopped)
1 tsp jaggery
2 tbsp chopped coriander leaves
Salt to taste

For The Vaghar
1 tbsp oil
½ tsp mustard seeds
¼ tsp cummin seeds
A pinch of asafoetida
12 curry leaves

METHOD

Wash and chop the tomatoes. Add water and pressure cook till soft (i.e. after 1 whistle, pressure cook on a low flame for about 3 minutes). When the pressure cooker is opened, cool the tomatoes and pass them through a sieve.

Reheat the tomato juice. Add the salt, coconut, green chillies and jaggery. Cook uncovered on a low flame for about 5 minutes. Remove from heat and keep covered.

Heat the oil. Add the mustard seeds, cummin seeds and asafoetida. When the mustard seeds splutter, add the curry leaves and pour quickly into the Tomato Saar. Cover immediately. Garnish with coriander leaves.

Serve hot with rice.

SERVES : 4-6

Usal Pav
White Peas with Bread

This spicy concoction, although quite simple and straightforward to prepare, is very popular and versatile. It can be used as a snack, a meal-in-a-dish, a light meal or as one of the dishes with a regular meal. The main accompaniment to this dish is long thin slices of onion mixed with finely chopped green chillies and coriander leaves.

INGREDIENTS

1½ cups dry white peas
2 tbsp oil
1 medium-sized onion (peeled & chopped)
1 tsp ginger paste
1½ tsp garlic paste
½ tsp turmeric powder
¼ cup tamarind juice
½ tsp garam masala
¼ cup chopped coriander leaves
Salt to taste

For The Masala Paste
1 tbsp oil
1 medium-sized onion
½ cup grated coconut
2 tsp coriander seeds
2 cloves
2 cardamoms
1 Bay leaf
6 peppercorns
6 red chillies
1" stick cinnamon
1 tsp poppy seeds

Accompaniments
12 small pav buns
3 medium-sized onions
(peeled & cut into long thin slices)
2 tbsp green chillies (chopped)
¼ cup chopped coriander leaves

METHOD

Pick, wash and soak the peas overnight in water. Add salt and pressure cook till soft(i.e. after 1 whistle, pressure cook on a low flame for about 5 minutes). Remove from heat and set aside.

Next, prepare the gravy. Heat the oil. With the exception of the onion and coconut, fry all the ingredients mentioned under Masala Paste together for about 3 minutes. Drain. Add the onion and coconut and fry till brown. Add ½ cup water, little by little, and grind all the masala ingredients together to make a smooth paste. Set aside.

Heat 2 tablespoons oil. Add the onion and fry until light brown in colour. Add the ginger and garlic and fry for 1 minute. Add the ground masala paste, salt, boiled peas, turmeric powder and tamarind juice. Bring to a boil. Cook uncovered on a medium flame for about 5 minutes, making sure there is plenty of gravy. Add the garam masala. Garnish with coriander leaves.

Serve hot accompanied by small pav buns and slices of onion mixed with chopped green chillies and coriander leaves.

SERVES : 4-6

Parsi

Akoori
Scrambled Eggs

Scrambled eggs are prepared in the traditional Parsi style. This dish is generally served as a Sunday breakfast with toast.
The main accompaniment to this dish is toast.

INGREDIENTS

3 tbsp oil
1 cup chopped onion
1 tsp cummin seeds
6 green chillies (chopped)
6 cloves garlic
½ tsp turmeric powder
1 tsp sugar
1 tbsp chopped green raw mango (optional)
1 large tomato (chopped)
6 tbsp chopped coriander leaves
6 eggs
Salt to taste

METHOD

Heat the oil and add the onion. Fry on a low flame stirring often. When the onion becomes light brown, add the cummin seeds, green chillies, garlic, turmeric powder and salt. Fry for 2 minutes. Add the sugar, raw mango, tomato and 4 tablespoons coriander leaves. Fry for a minute. Beat the eggs with a little salt and add to the fried mixture. Stir briskly for about 3 minutes over a high flame. Add the remaining 2 tablespoons coriander leaves.

Serve hot on toast or along with toast for breakfast.

SERVES : 4-6

90

Dhansak
Mixed Lentils, Vegetable and Mutton Curry

This is one of the best and most popular Parsi dishes and is generally served for Sunday lunch with Dhansak Rice.

INGREDIENTS

500 gms mutton
2 cups toovar dal
¼ cup masoor dal
¼ cup yellow mung dal
¼ cup val dal
1 cup chopped onion
1 tbsp chopped ginger
1 tbsp chopped garlic
¼ cup chopped red pumpkin
1 cup chopped brinjal
½ potato (chopped)
1 cup chopped sweet potato
1 medium-sized bunch fenugreek leaves (chopped)
½ cup chopped coriander leaves
5 cups water
6 cloves
½" piece cinnamon
4 Kashmiri chillies
8 peppercorns
1 tsp coriander seeds
1 tsp cummin seeds
¾ tsp turmeric powder
Salt to taste

For The Vagshar
3 tbsp oil
1 cup chopped onion
1 medium-sized tomato (chopped)

For Garnishing
1 tsp dry methi leaves

METHOD

Clean, wash and cut the mutton into medium-sized pieces. Pick, wash and soak all the dals together in 3 cups of water. Set aside for about 30 minutes.

Combine the mutton and the dals along with the water in which they were soaked, the onion, ginger, garlic, red pumpkin, brinjal, potato, sweet potato, fenugreek leaves, coriander leaves, the remaining 2 cups of water and salt. Pressure cook till everything is nicely cooked (i.e. after 1 whistle, pressure cook on a low flame for about 15 minutes). When the pressure cooker is opened, remove the mutton pieces and put them aside separately. Mash the dals and vegetable mixture with an egg beater or run in a liquidiser. Set aside.

Heat 3 tablespoons oil separately and fry the onion on a low flame, stirring often. When the onion becomes brown, add the ground masala powder or readymade Dhansak masala and the tomato. Fry for about 3 minutes. Add the mashed dal and vegetable mixture and the mutton. Bring to a boil. Cook uncovered on a low flame for about 7 minutes. Sprinkle dry methi leaves on top. Serve hot with Dhansak Rice.

If assorted dals not handy, use 1¼ cups toovar dal.

SERVES : 4-6

Patrani Macchi

Fish in Banana Leaves

A real delicacy. It is as beautiful to behold as it is tasty to the palate.
This dish is generally served at wedding dinners and other days of
celebration. Before steaming the banana parcels, pay special attention to
the sprinkling of vinegar, as this imparts an unusual flavour to the dish.
The main accompaniment to this dish is chappatis.

INGREDIENTS

2 medium-sized pomfrets
Juice of 2 medium-sized lemons
10 pieces of banana leaves
(each cut into 7" x 7" squares)
2 cups water
½ cup oil
¼ cup vinegar
Salt to taste

For The Masala
1 cup grated coconut
8 green chillies
8 cloves garlic
1 ½ cups coriander leaves   Grind
2 tbsp mint leaves   to a
1 tsp cummin seeds   paste
Juice of 1 medium-sized lemon
1 tsp sugar
Salt to taste

METHOD

Cut each pomfret into 5 pieces and make 3 short slits on the surface of each side. Wash, clean and apply lemon juice and salt all over the fish pieces and set aside for about 20 minutes. Drain from the lemon and salt liquid and pat dry with a clean napkin. Apply the ground masala paste all over the fish pieces and put some in the slits.

Boil the water in a broad vessel. Remove from heat. Dip each banana leaf quickly and carefully into the hot water and drain immediately. Pat dry each leaf with a clean napkin. Wrap each piece of masala-coated fish in a banana leaf and tie with a string. Arrange all the banana parcels in a single layer in a sieve. Heat the oil and sprinkle over the banana parcels. Then sprinkle the vinegar.

Steam for about 20 minutes. If you wish, instead of steaming, you may bake the fish for about 30 minutes in a moderate oven (350°F).

There is yet another method. Heat the oil in a thick-bottomed pan. Arrange the banana parcels in a single layer. Sprinkle the vinegar on the banana parcels. Cover the pan. Put some water on the lid of the pan. Cook for 10 minutes on a low flame. Turn over the banana parcels. Cook in the same manner for 10 minutes. If the banana leaves turn dark, it means that the fish is ready. Serve hot as one of the dishes for lunch or dinner.

If banana leaves are not handy, use foil.

SERVES : 4-6

Saas Ni Machhi
Fish in Sauce

This dish is relished because of its sweet, sour and spicy sauce. While adding the eggs, vinegar and sugar, always keep the flame low and be very quick and careful in order to prevent the eggs from getting lumpy and spoiling the sauce. The main accompaniment to this dish is chappatis or khichri.

INGREDIENTS

10 medium-sized pieces of pomfret
4 tbsp oil
½ tsp cummin seeds
2 medium-sized onions (peeled & chopped)
3 green chillies ⎫
1" piece ginger ⎬ Grind together
8 cloves garlic ⎬
2 medium-sized tomatoes ⎬
¼ cup coriander leaves ⎭
1 tbsp gram flour
3 cups water
¼ tsp turmeric powder
Salt to taste

For Mixing Together
2 beaten eggs
1 tbsp vinegar
I tbsp sugar
¼ tsp pepper

For Garnishing
3 tbsp chopped coriander leaves

To Apply On The Fish Pieces
1 tbsp vinegar or lemon juice
A little salt

METHOD

Wash the fish and apply vinegar and salt. Set aside. Heat the oil in a pan. Add the cummin seeds. When the cummin seeds become red, add the onion and fry on a low flame, stirring often. Add the ground masala and gram flour. Fry on a medium flame for 3 minutes. Add the water, turmeric powder and salt. Bring to a boil. Cook covered on a low flame for about 5 minutes.

Add the fish pieces. Cook covered on a low flame for about 7-10 minutes or until the fish is cooked. Turn just once in-between. Keep the flame low and add the egg, vinegar, sugar and pepper mixture. Stir continuously for about 2 minutes, making sure there are no lumps and the fish pieces do not break. Garnish with coriander leaves.

Serve hot with chappatis or khichri.

SERVES : 4-6

Doodh Powva

Beaten Rice in Milk

A very unusual, delectable and nourishing dessert.
Moreover, it is so quick and easy to prepare.

INGREDIENTS

½ cup poha (beaten rice)
3 cups milk
3½ tbsp sugar
3 crushed cardamoms
¼ tsp nutmeg
1 tbsp raisins
12 almonds(blanched & cut into
long thin pieces)
½ tsp vanilla essence

METHOD

Pick and wash the poha. Set aside.

Boil the milk. Add the sugar and stir till the sugar dissolves. Cook uncovered on a low flame for about 5 minutes, stirring often. Add the cardamoms, nutmeg powder and poha. Cook uncovered on a low flame, stirring most of the time, for about 10 minutes, or until the mixture becomes thick. Add the raisins and almonds. Simmer uncovered for 2 minutes. Remove from heat and cool at room temperature.

Add the vanilla essence and mix well. Place on a refrigerator shelf until well chilled.

Serve cold as a dessert.

SERVES : 4-6

Dhansak Rice
Pulao for Dhansak

An excellent traditional pulao which is generally served with Dhansak curry for Sunday lunch.

INGREDIENTS

1½ cups short-grained rice (Surti Kolam)
3 cups water
1 tbsp sugar
2 tbsp oil
4 cloves
½" piece cinnamon
2 cardamoms
8 peppercorns
1 cup long thin slices of onion
Salt to taste

METHOD

Pick, wash and soak the rice in 2½ cups water for about 30 minutes. Dissolve the sugar very carefully in a pan placed over a low flame until it turns golden brown but not burnt. Add ½ cup water, stir well, bring to a boil, remove the pan from the flame and set aside.

Heat the oil in a thick-bottomed pan. Add the cloves, cinnamon, cardamoms and peppercorns. Stir quickly and add the onion. Fry on a low flame, stirring often, until the onion becomes light brown. Add the rice after draining it and fry over a medium flame for about 5 minutes, stirring often.

Add the sugar water, 2½ cups of water in which the rice was soaked and salt. Bring to a boil. Reduce the flame to low and cook covered for about 15 minutes or until the rice is cooked, stirring a few times very carefully, so that the rice does not get mashed.

Serve hot with Dhansak.

Laganshala Stew
Mixed Vegetable Stew

As the name implies, this is a delicacy served at Parsi wedding lunches and dinners. The main accompaniment to this dish is chappatis or bread.

INGREDIENTS

2 medium-sized sweet potatoes
2 potatoes
2 carrots
10 French beans
Oil for frying
1 medium-sized onion (peeled & chopped)
2 green chillies ⎤
1" piece ginger ⎬ Grind to a paste
6 cloves garlic ⎦
2 medium-sized tomatoes (chopped)
15 curry leaves
1 tsp coriander powder
1 tsp cummin powder
½ tsp chilli powder
½ tsp turmeric powder
1/4 cup water
1 tsp sugar
1 tbsp vinegar
1 tsp Worcestershire sauce (optional)
Salt to taste

METHOD

Peel the sweet potatoes and potatoes. Scrape the carrots. String the French beans. Cut the sweet potatoes, potatoes and carrots into small cubes. Cut the French beans into ½" long pieces. Keep each vegetable separate. Wash all the vegetables separately and drain well.

Heat the oil in a frying pan. Fry each vegetable separately. Drain and set aside together.

Heat the oil in a frying pan. Add the onion and fry on a low flame, stirring often, until the onion becomes brown. Add the ground paste and fry for a minute. Add the tomatoes, curry leaves, coriander powder, cummin powder, chilli powder, turmeric powder, water, fried vegetables, salt and sugar. Cook covered on a low flame for about 5 minutes or until almost dry. Add vinegar and Worcestershire sauce, then stir.

Serve hot with chappatis or bread.

SERVES : 4-6

Lagan Nu Custard
Wedding Custard

A rich and delicious baked or steamed pudding. As the name implies, it is generally served at weddings as a dessert. Make sure the milk is absolutely cold before adding the eggs, so that the eggs do not get lumpy and spoil the custard.

INGREDIENTS

3 cups milk
6 tbsp sugar
2 crushed cardamoms
$^1/_8$ tsp crushed nutmeg
3 eggs
¼ tsp vanilla essence
6 almonds (blanched & chopped)
6 pistachio nuts (blanched & chopped)
1 tsp pumpkin seeds (optional)

METHOD

Boil the milk. Add the sugar and stir until the sugar dissolves.

Cook uncovered on a low flame for about 20 minutes, stirring continuously, so that the milk becomes quite thick. Remove from heat and add the cardamoms and nutmeg.

Cool the prepared milk thoroughly at room temperature.

Break the eggs in a separate bowl and beat with a fork. Add the eggs to the prepared milk along with the vanilla essence and the nuts. Pour the mixture into a greased baking dish, making sure the dish is not filled to the brim, as the custard will rise while baking. Sprinkle the remaining nuts on top of the custard. Bake the custard in a pre-heated moderately hot oven (350⁰F) for about 20-30 minutes, or until the custard is well set and the top is brown. Cool the custard at room temperature, turn out from baking dish and then refrigerate. Cut into slices and serve cold as a dessert.

If you wish, instead of baking, you may steam the custard, duly covered, in a pressure **cooker**, for about 15 minutes.

SERVES : 4-6

Ravo

Semolina Sweet

*This sweet is generally served on Parsi New Year's Day
and other days of celebration.*

INGREDIENTS

1½ tbsp melted ghee
2 tbsp fine semolina (sooji or rava)
3 cups milk
3 tbsp sugar

For Garnishing
¼ tsp crushed cardamoms
¼ tsp crushed nutmeg
1 tbsp raisins
8 almonds(blanched & cut into
long thin pieces)

METHOD

Heat the ghee and lightly fry the raisins and almonds. Remove from the ghee and set aside.

In the same ghee, fry the semolina on a low flame, stirring continuously, for about 3 minutes or until it turns light brown. Add the milk gradually and cook on a low flame, stirring continuously, for about 5 minutes. Add the sugar and cook in the same manner for about 10 minutes or until the mixture becomes thick but not too dry. It should be of a semi-solid consistency.

Pour the prepared Ravo into a serving dish. Garnish with cardamom, nutmeg, fried raisins and almonds.

Serve hot or cold for breakfast or as a dessert. For cold ravo, refrigerate for some time.

SERVES : 4-6

Punjabi

Kheema Mutter

Minced Meat with Green Peas

The green peas and the flavour of the spices create an appetitising dish.
Moreover, an easy method is used to prepare this dish.
The main accompaniments to it are chappatis,
tandoori rotis, naans or rice.

INGREDIENTS

1 large onion (peeled & grated)
1 tbsp chopped green chillies } Grind
1 tsp chopped ginger   } to a
1 tsp chopped garlic   } paste
2 large tomatoes(immersed in hot water
for 5 minutes, drained, peeled & chopped)
500 gms minced meat
1 cup shelled green peas
½ tsp turmeric powder
2 tsp coriander powder
½ tsp chilli powder
1 cup water
½ tsp garam masala
¼ cup chopped coriander leaves
Salt to taste

METHOD

Heat the oil. Add the onion and fry till golden brown. Add the ground paste and fry for a minute. Add the tomatoes and cook covered for 2 minutes. Mash lightly. Add the minced meat. Fry on a medium flame for about 5 minutes, stirring most of the time.

Add the green peas, turmeric powder, coriander powder and chilli powder. Stir. Add the water and salt. Pressure cook till done (i.e. after 1 whistle, pressure cook on a low flame for about 3 minutes). When the pressure cooker is opened, cook uncovered on a low flame for about 3 minutes. Add the garam masala. Stir. Garnish with coriander leaves.

Serve hot with chappatis, tandoori rotis, naans or rice.

SERVES : 4-6

Palak Gosht
Mutton with Spinach

Spinach forms a delightful combination with mutton and makes this preparation distinctive and nutritious. The main accompaniments to this dish are chappatis, tandoori rotis, naans or rice.

INGREDIENTS

For The Spinach
2 medium-sized bunches of spinach
½ cup water
Salt to taste

For the Mutton
500 gms lean mutton
(cut into 1" x 1" squares)
3 tbsp oil
½ tsp cummin seeds
1 medium-sized onion (peeled & grated)
3 green chillies ⎤
1" piece ginger ⎬ Grind to a paste using a little water
8 cloves garlic ⎦
1 tbsp coriander powder
¾ tsp turmeric powder
1 tsp chilii powder
½ cup fresh curd (beaten)
¼ cup water
½ tsp garam masala
1 tbsp lemon juice
Salt to taste

METHOD

Clean the spinach and cut it into large pieces. Wash it in plenty of water. Drain and add ½ cup water and salt. Cook uncovered in a pan for 3 minutes. Drain the spinach in a bowl of ice cold water. Set the spinach water aside. Then remove the spinach from the cold water and grind to a fine paste. Set aside.

Next prepare the mutton. Heat the oil and add the cummin seeds. Then add the onion and fry on a low flame for about 3 minutes, stirring often. Add the ground paste and fry for a minute. Add the mutton and fry for about 5 minutes, stirring often. Add the coriander powder, turmeric powder, chilli powder and curd. Fry for about 2 minutes. Add salt, water and the spinach water. Pressure cook till the mutton is almost tender (i.e. after 1 whistle, pressure cook on a slow fire for about 5 minutes). When the pressure cooker is opened, add the ground spinach and cook uncovered over a medium flame for a few minutes, until the mixture is almost dry. Add the garam masala and lemon juice.

Serve hot with chappatis, puris, tandoori rotis or naans.

SERVES : 4-6

Seekh Kabab
Skewered Kababs

A real delicacy, extremely popular during a barbecue or a snack party. Make sure the raw meat used is completely dry, as otherwise, it will fall off the skewer while roasting. The main accompaniments to this dish are coriander chutney, thin round slices of onion and small pieces of lemon.

INGREDIENTS

500 gms minced meat (kheema)
2 tsp chopped ginger
1 tsp chopped garlic
2 tsp chopped green chillies
¼ cup chopped coriander leaves
Juice of a medium-sized lemon
1 tbsp dry fenugreek leaves (kasoori methi)
1 tsp poppy seeds
1 tsp chilli powder
½ tsp garam masala
1 tbsp cornflour or gram flour
½ tsp orange-red food colouring
1 egg
A little oil
Salt to taste

For The Accompaniments
3 medium-sized onions
(peeled & cut into thin rounds)
3 medium-sized lemons
(cut into 4 pieces each)
Coriander chutney

METHOD

Do not wash the minced meat. With the exception of the egg and oil, add all the remaining ingredients to the minced meat. Grind to a smooth mixture. Add the egg to the ground mixture and keep covered in the refrigerator for 2 hours.

Grease the skewers with a pastry brush or muslin cloth dipped in oil. With moist hands, press small portions of the meat mixture onto the skewers, making thin 4" long rolls.

Roast the kababs on a charcoal fire, (tandoor), hot grill or even the open flame of a gas burner, for a few minutes, until the kababs turn light brown all over. While roasting, turn the skewers very slowly and carefully, as otherwise the mixture may fall off. Brush a little oil all over and roast further for about 5 minutes or until the kababs turn golden brown. Remove from heat and slide the kababs off the skewers onto a serving dish.

Serve hot with cocktails or as a snack, starter or side dish to a meal, accompanied by sliced onion, lemon pieces and coriander chutney.

SERVES : 4-6

Tandoori Murgi
Baked Chicken

This mouth-watering delicacy, which few can resist, has won international fame. It is the in-thing at parties. Marinating the chicken pieces is a must in this preparation, as this helps to soften the chicken, thereby reducing the cooking time and above all, enhances the taste due to penetration of the masala.

INGREDIENTS

1 medium-sized tender chicken
(approx 700 gms, preferably a broiler)
1 medium-sized onion ⎤
2 green chillies   ⎥ Grind
1" piece ginger   ⎬ to a
10 cloves garlic   ⎥ paste
1 cup fresh curd   ⎦
1 tbsp coriander powder
1 tsp garam masala
½ tsp orange-red food colouring
½ cup oil
Salt to taste

**Masala For Sprinkling
On The Chicken Pieces After Grilling**
1½ tsp roasted cummin powder ⎤
1 tsp chilli powder (optional) ⎥ Masala
1 tsp mango powder   ⎬ A
Salt to taste   ⎦

For Garnishing
1 medium-sized onion (peeled & cut
into rounds)
1 big lemon (cut into 8 pieces)
8 green chillies (kept whole)
1" piece ginger (scraped & cut into
long thin pieces)

METHOD

Clean, wash and dry the chicken with a clean napkin. Cut it into 10 or 12 pieces. Mix the ground paste, curd, coriander powder, garam masala, salt and colouring. Apply this mixture all over the chicken pieces and set aside for 6 hours or leave overnight in the refrigerator. Apply oil on the marinated chicken pieces.

Grill the chicken pieces on coals or under an electric or gas grill or cook in a gas oven. You can also bake the chicken pieces in a greased baking dish in a moderately hot oven for about 30 minutes. Make sure the pieces are uniformly brown and tender on both sides. Grill or bake the chicken pieces for the first 20 minutes on high heat and the remaining 10 minutes on low heat, basting with the remaining marinade.

When ready, sprinkle the Masala (marked A) on the chicken pieces and garnish with the onion, lemon, green chillies and ginger.

Serve immediately with tandoori rotis, naans, chappatis or as a cocktail snack or starter.

SERVES : 4-6

Tawa Murgi

Chicken prepared on a Griddle

A very convenient method of preparing chicken on a tawa which makes the chicken pieces very crisp. It also has a wonderful flavour imparted by the green chillies.

INGREDIENTS

12 medium-sized pieces of tender chicken

For The Marinade
1 medium-sized onion
2 green chillies
1" piece ginger
10 cloves garlic
1 cup fresh curd
1 tbsp coriander powder
1 tsp garam masala
½ tsp orange-red food colouring
Salt to taste

For Frying
12 green chillies
(slit lengthwise)
Oil

Masala For Sprinkling On The Chicken Pieces After Frying
1½ tsp roasted cummin powder
1 tbsp chilli powder (optional)
1 tsp mango powder
Salt to taste

For Garnishing
1 medium-sized onion
(peeled & cut into thin round slices)
1 large lemon (cut into 8 pieces)
1" piece ginger (scraped & cut into long thin pieces)

METHOD

Combine all the ingredients mentioned under Marinade. Apply this mixture all over the chicken pieces and set aside for 6 hours or leave overnight in the refrigerator.

Fry the chicken pieces just before serving. For this, heat 4 tablespoons oil on a griddle (tawa) and add 4 chicken pieces. Fry uncovered on a low flame for about 10 minutes. Then turn over, add 8 green chilli halves and fry the other sides of the chicken pieces for 10 minutes. Fry the remaining chicken pieces in a single layer in a serving dish. Sprinkle the masala all over the chicken pieces. Garnish with the onion, lemon and ginger pieces.

Serve very hot with tandoori rotis, naans, chappatis or as a cocktails snack or starter or side dish to a meal.

SERVES : 4-6

Aloo Raita
Potatoes with Curd Sauce

A popular nutritious accompaniment to a vegetarian meal, intended to balance the spices in other dishes.

INGREDIENTS

1 cup chopped boiled potatoes
¼ tsp chilli powder (optional)
1½ cups fresh thick curd
¼ cup water
¼ tsp pepper
¼ tsp roasted cummin powder
2 tbsp chopped mint leaves
4 tbsp chopped coriander leaves
Salt to taste

METHOD

Add salt and chilli powder to the chopped potatoes, mix well and set aside.

Beat the curd with an egg beater or churner for about 3 minutes. Add water and beat again for about 3 minutes, so as to obtain a smooth consistency. Add salt, pepper and roasted cummin powder. Stir. Add the prepared boiled potatoes. Mix well and pour into a glass bowl. Garnish with chopped mint and coriander leaves. Place the bowl in the refrigerator .

Serve cold with parathas, pulao or as an accompaniment to a meal.

SERVES : 4-6

Baigan Bharta
Mashed Brinjal

The salient feature of this dish is the roasting of the brinjal which gives it such an extraordinary taste that even those averse to this vegetable will enjoy eating it. The main accompaniments to this dish are chappatis, tandoori rotis, naans or parathas.

INGREDIENTS

1 large brinjal (approx 400 gms)
2 tbsp oil
A pinch of asafoetida
½ tsp cummin seeds
1 large onion (peeled & chopped)
1 tbsp chopped ginger
1 tsp chopped garlic
1 tsp chopped green chillies
1 large tomato (chopped)
1 tsp chilli powder
½ tsp turmeric powder
½ tsp garam masala
Salt to taste

For Garnishing
3 tbsp chopped coriander leaves
2 green chillies, kept whole

METHOD

Wash and wipe the brinjal. Roast it over an open gas flame for a few minutes, turning it often to expose the entire brinjal to the heat. When the brinjal shrinks and becomes soft and its peel turns black, stop roasting. Cool, peel and mash the brinjal.

Heat the oil in a pan. Add the asafoetida and cummin seeds. Stir. Add ½ the onion, ginger, garlic and green chillies. Fry on a low flame for about 5 minutes, stirring often. Add the tomato, mashed brinjal, chilli powder, turmeric powder and salt. Cook covered on a low flame for about 5 minutes. Mash the brinjal thoroughly with the back of a ladle and add the remaining onion. Cook uncovered on a high flame for 2 minutes, stirring continuously. Add the garam masala. Mix well. Transfer the bharta to a serving dish. Garnish with coriander leaves and green chillies.

Serve hot with chappatis, tandoori rotis, naans or parathas.

SERVES : 4-6

Bharwan Bhindi
Stuffed Lady's Fingers

Stuffed vegetables enjoy a high degree of popularity and are considered a real treat. This dish is a favourite with even the most fastidious eater. Do not stir the lady's fingers too often and handle them gently, as otherwise, they may break and look unappetising. The main accompaniments to this dish are chappatis, tandoori rotis, naans or parathas.

INGREDIENTS

400 gms more or less equal-sized lady's fingers
3 tbsp oil
A pinch of asafoetida
1 tsp cummin seeds
½ tsp turmeric powder

For The Stuffing
2 tbsp oil
2 tbsp coriander powder
1 tbsp chilli powder
1 tsp turmeric powder
I tsp mango powder
½ tsp garam masala
1 tsp ginger paste (optional)
1 tsp garlic paste (optional)
Salt to taste

METHOD

Wash the lady's fingers and wipe them with a clean napkin. Cut off both ends of each lady's finger. Slit the lady's fingers one by one, lengthwise, almost all the way, on one side only, keeping them intact.

Combine all the ingredients mentioned under Stuffing. Stuff the lady's fingers with this mixture.

Heat the oil in a broad pan. Add the asafoetida and cummin seeds. Stir. Add the stuffed lady's fingers. Cook covered on a low flame for about 15 minutes or until the lady's fingers are cooked. Stir a few times in-between very carefully, so that the lady's fingers do not break.

Serve hot with chappatis.

Chhole Bhature

White Gram with Leavened Fried Bread

This delicious and sustaining dish is justly famous. It is excellent as a snack or as a meal-in-a-dish. After preparing the bhatura dough, ensure that it is set aside for about 8 hours, duly covered with a muslin cloth (this prevents skin formation on the surface of the dough). Setting aside allows the dough to increase in volume as a result of which the bhaturas become light.

INGREDIENTS

For The Chhole
As mentioned in the recipe
Punjabi Chhole

For The Bhaturas
1½ cups refined flour
½ cup sour curd
A pinch of soda bi carbonate
A pinch of salt
Oil for frying
A little water for mixing

METHOD

Combine the refined flour, soda bi carbonate and salt. Add the curd and mix well. Add very little water, knead and prepare a pliable dough. Cover with a muslin cloth and set aside in a warm place either overnight or for at least 8 hours, so that the dough rises.

Make small balls from the dough, flatten them on the palm or roll out like thick puris, approximately 4" in diameter.

Heat the oil to smoking point in a frying pan and deep fry the bhaturas on a low flame until they turn light brown. Drain and set aside. When serving, heat the bhaturas on a tawa, using very little oil and serve hot with Punjabi Chhole.

This dish can be served as a snack or as a small meal by itself.

SERVES : 4-6

Dal Fry
Lentils with Special Tempering

The vaghar added to the cooked dal, preferably just before serving, not only makes it more appealing to look at but also lends a special flavour and taste. Moreover, Dal Fry is very sustaining and satisfying. The main accompaniment to this dish are chappatis or rice.

INGREDIENTS

1 cup toovar dal
2½ cups water
½ tsp turmeric powder
Salt to taste

For The Vaghar
3 tbsp oil
¾ cup chopped onion
1 tsp chopped garlic
1 tsp chopped ginger
1 tsp chopped green chillies
½ tsp cummin seeds
A pinch of asafoetida
1 medium-sized tomato (cut into small pieces)
1 tsp chilli powder
¼ tsp turmeric powder
Salt to taste

For Garnishing
¼ cup chopped coriander leaves

METHOD

Pick, wash and soak the dal in 2½ cups of water for about 30 minutes. Pressure cook till the dal is done (i.e. after 1 whistle, pressure cook on a low flame for about 2 minutes).

When the pressure cooker is opened, reheat the dal and cook uncovered on a medium flame for 2 minutes. Do not mash the dal. Remove from heat and keep covered.

Heat the oil. Add the onion, garlic, ginger, green chillies and cummin seeds. Fry on a medium flame for about 4 minutes, stirring often. Add the remaining ingredients mentioned under Vaghar and fry on a high flame for 2 minutes. Remove from heat. Add ½ of this mixture to the hot cooked dal. Stir the dal. Set aside the remaining ½ of the vaghar mixture aside. When serving, reheat the dal. Pour into a serving dish. Put in the vaghar mixture that was set aside. Garnish with coriander leaves.

Note : For best results, just before serving, reheat the dal well, pour in a serving dish, prepare the vaghar and pour on top of the dal. Do not stir.

SERVES : 4-6

Maharani Dal
Queen of Lentils

A classic dish, yet so simple to prepare. The butter and cream make it rich and aromatic and fit for a special occasion. The main accompaniments to this dish are chappatis, tandoori rotis, naans or rice.

INGREDIENTS

For The Dal
1 cup whole black beans (saabat urad)
2 tbsp red kidney beans (rajmah)
1 tbsp Bengal gram
6 cups water
1 tbsp chopped ginger
1 tsp chopped garlic
1 tsp turmeric powder
½ tsp chilli powder
2 medium-sized tomatoes (immersed in hot water for 5 minutes, drained, peeled & chopped)
1 tbsp softened butter
2 tbsp fresh cream (beaten)
Salt to taste

For The Vaghar
1 tbsp oil
½ tsp cummin seeds
1 tbsp chopped green chillies
$1/_3$ tsp chopped ginger
½ tsp chopped garlic
¼ tsp chilli powder
½ tsp garam masala

For Garnishing
½ cup (chopped)coriander leaves
1 tbsp grated ginger
2 whole green chillies (slit into two vertically through the centre)

METHOD

Pick, wash and soak the whole urad, and chana dal together in 6 cups of water either overnight or at least for 8 hours. Add the ginger, garlic, turmeric powder, chilli powder and salt. Pressure cook till soft and creamy (i.e. after 1 whistle, pressure cook on a low flame for about 15 minutes).

When the pressure cooker is opened, add the tomatoes, butter and cream. Cook uncovered on a low flame for about 10 minutes, mashing the mixture lightly till the dal becomes creamy. Heat the oil in a separate pan. Add the rest of the ingredients mentioned under Vaghar. Fry quickly and add to the cooked dal. Mix well. Pour into a serving dish. Garnish with coriander leaves, ginger and green chillies.

Serve hot with chappatis, tandoori rotis, naans or rice.

SERVES : 4-6

Gajar Ki Kanji
Carrot Appetiser

A beautiful nourishing and appetising drink, generally prepared in the winter months. Here is an unusual way to consume carrots, which have high Vitamin A content which aids vision.

INGREDIENTS

2 medium-sized carrots
1 small beetroot
6 cups of drinking water
3 tsp mustard powder
1 tsp chillie powder
Salt to taste

METHOD

Scrape the carrots and peel the beetroot. Wash the whole carrots and beetroot. Chop the carrots and the beetroot into 1" long pieces. Measure both separately to make approximately 1 cup of carrots and ½ cup of beetroot.

Take a glass or earthenware jar and pour the drinking water into it. Add the chopped carrots and beetroot along with the mustard powder, chilli powder and salt. Stir and close the jar properly. Set aside for about 3 days, stirring at least once a day. The Kanji will be almost ready on the third day and just right on the fourth day. Stir and serve the Carrot Kanji in individual glass bowls, with a tablespoon, either at the beginning or a meal or along with a meal. As the taste of the carrots and beetroot will be absorbed by the liquid, the liquid is more important than the pieces of carrots and beetroot. This liquid is known as Kanji and is a very good appetiser. While drinking the Carrot Kanji, a few pieces of carrot and beetroot can also be eaten.

This Carrot Kanji is usually prepared in the winter months and is therefore quite cool at room temperature. However, the Carrot Kanji can be chilled in a refrigerator and served cold if preferred.

SERVES : 4-6

Gobhi Musallam
Whole Cauliflower

A sumptuous vegetarian delight that outbests most non-vegetarian dishes. A joy to the eyes and palate. Excellent for a party. While deep frying the cauliflower, make sure that it is firm and never overcooked and soggy. Overcooking will ruin the dish both in appearance and taste. The main accompaniments are either chappatis, tandoori rotis, naans or parathas.

INGREDIENTS

500 gms cauliflower (preferably two small cauliflower heads of 250 gms each)
Oil for deep frying
2 medium-sized potatoes
(each peeled & cut into 8 pieces)
1 cup chopped onion
1 tsp chopped garlic
1 tbsp chopped ginger
1 tbsp chopped green chillies
3 medium-sized tomatoes
(chopped into small pieces)
6 peppercorns
1 medium-sized bay leaf
½" piece cinnamon
1 cardamom
2 cloves
1 tbsp coriander powder
¾ tsp turmeric powder
1 tsp chilli powder
¾ tsp garam masala
½ cup water
Salt to taste

For Garnishing
12 cashewnut halves
1 tbsp raisins
½ cup coriander leaves

METHOD

Clean and wash the whole cauliflower heads. Do not discard the tender leaves and stalks. Chop these into small pieces and set aside separately.

Apply a little salt to the cauliflower and potato pieces and set aside separately for 5 minutes. Heat the oil and deep fry the cashewnuts and raisins. Drain and set aside. Deep fry the whole cauliflower heads and potato pieces separately till they turn light brown colour, over a medium flame. Drain and set aside.

Heat 4 tablespoons oil in a thick broad pan. Add the onion, garlic, ginger and green chillies. Fry on a low flame for about 3 minutes, stirring often. Add the tomatoes, cauliflower leaves and stalks and fry in the same manner for about 5 minutes. Add the peppercorns, Bay leaf, cinnamon, cardamom, cloves, coriander powder, turmeric powder, chilli powder and garam masala. Stir quickly. Add water and salt. Bring to a boil and add the fried cauliflower heads and potatoes. Cook covered on a low flame for about 5 to 7 minutes or until dry, stirring once or twice carefully. Garnish with cashewnuts, raisins and coriander leaves.

Serve hot with chappatis, naans or tandoori rotis.

SERVES : 4-6

Gulabi Burfi
Rose Flavoured Milk Sweet

An easy method is used to prepare this beautiful pink burfi with a rose flavour. This dish is generally made during festivals like Diwali, Dassera, Raksha Bandhan or other days of celebration, when it may be garnished with almonds and silver leaf (vark). While adding the sugar, knead the mawa very well so that there are absolutely no cracks. The presence of cracks can ruin the look of the dish and result in the disintegration of the pieces while cutting them.

INGREDIENTS

1 cup solidified milk (mawa) approx 100 gms
½ cup powdered sugar
A little rose essence
A little cochineal colouring
2 tbsp tiny pieces of cashewnuts or walnuts

METHOD

Knead the mawa well to remove any lumps. Warm the mawa in a non-stick pan on a low flame for about 2 minutes, stirring continuously. Remove from heat and cool thoroughly at room temperature.

Add the powdered sugar, essence and colouring to the cold mawa and knead thoroughly by hand, so that there are no cracks. Arrange the prepared mawa in a flat greased plate, to a thickness of ½" and a width of 1". Press in the cashewnuts or walnuts throughout the central area of the mawa. Set aside for an hour or so to dry. Then cut into 1" x 1" squares and store.

SERVES : 4-6

Hara Bara Kabab
Green Kababs

These green kababs are so stunning both in appearance and taste that they have rightly become a delicacy. The main accompaniment to this dish is Coriander Chutney.

INGREDIENTS

1 cup mashed or grated cottage cheese, approx 100 gms
4 cups chopped spinach leaves
2 cups water
2 slices bread, soaked in water, drained & squeezed (approx 1 cup mashed)
1 tsp green chilli paste
½ tsp garlic paste
1 tsp ginger paste
Oil for frying
Salt to taste

METHOD

Wash the spinach leaves. Drain. Add 2 cups water. Cook uncovered in a pan for about 5 minutes. Drain the spinach in a bowl of ice cold water. Remove squeezing out water. Combine the spinach, cottage cheese, mashed bread, green chilli, garlic and ginger paste and salt. Grind to a smooth mixture without water. Place in a covered container and refrigerate for about 30 minutes to harden a bit.

Remove from the refrigerator. Divide this mixture into 12 equal portions. With slightly oily hands, form 2" long rolls or 2" diameter flat round kababs. Heat the oil in a frying pan. When the oil smokes, deep fry the kababs a few at a time. Drain when golden brown on both sides.

Serve hot as a snack, with cocktails or as starter or side dish to a meal, accompanied by chutney.

Makhani Sabzi
Vegetables in Butter

A simple method is used to prepare this lip smacking dish using butter, which richly enhances the taste. The main accompaniments are parathas, tandoori rotis, naans or toasts.

INGREDIENTS

3 tbsp butter
2 cups small pieces of mixed boiled veg-etables (carrots, French beans, potatoes & cauliflower)
¼ cup shelled boiled green peas
1 small capsicum(seeds removed & cut into 8 pieces)
2 tbsp fresh cream
¼ cup water
¼ tsp garam masala
2 tbsp chopped coriander leaves
Salt to taste

For The Masala Paste
2 tbsp oil
1 medium-sized onion (peeled & chopped)
1 tbsp chopped ginger
1 tsp chopped garlic
1 tbsp chopped green chillies
1 tsp chilli powder
2 cloves
½" stick cinnamon
2 cardamoms
2 tbsp small pieces of cashewnuts
1 tsp poppy seeds

METHOD

First prepare the Masala Paste. Heat the oil. Add the onion and fry on a low flame till it turns brown. Add the remaining ingredients mentioned under Masala Paste. Fry for 2 minutes, stirring continuously. Remove from heat, cool and grind to a fine paste. Set aside.

Melt the butter in a separate pan. Add the mixed boiled vegetables, green peas and capsicum. Fry on a medium flame for 2 minutes. Add the cream and masala paste. Fry for 3 minutes, stirring most of the time. Add the water, salt and garam masala. Cook uncovered on a high flame for 2 minutes. Garnish with coriander leaves.

Serve hot with tandoori rotis, naans, parathas or even toast.

SERVES : 4-6

Malai Koftas

Vegetable Balls in Rich Gravy

The balls in this curry are cooked in a gravy containing cream, which makes the dish both tasty and rich on account of which it is considered a real treat. Never overcook the gravy after adding the koftas, as this will make the koftas break. The main accompaniments are either chappatis, tandoori rotis, naans or parathas.

INGREDIENTS

For The Koftas
1 cup mashed or grated cottage cheese
4 medium-sized potatoes
(boiled, peeled & mashed)
2 slices bread (soaked in water, drained &
squeezed)
1 tbsp chopped green chillies
1 tsp chopped ginger ⎤ Grind
½ tbsp chopped garlic ⎬ to a
½ tsp cummin seeds ⎦ paste
Oil for frying
Salt to taste

For The Gravy
2 tbsp oil
1 tbsp chopped green chillies
1 tsp chopped ginger ⎤ Grind
1 tsp chopped garlic ⎬ to a
1 onion (peeled & chopped) ⎦ paste
2 tbsp cashewnut powder
½ tsp turmeric powder
½ tsp chilli powder
3 medium-sized tomatoes (immersed in hot
water for 5 minutes, drained, peeled &
chopped)
2 cups water
Salt to taste
½ cup fresh curd (beaten)
$^1/_3$ cup fresh cream (beaten)

½ tsp garam masala
¼ cup chopped coriander leaves

METHOD

First prepare the koftas. With the exception of the oil, combine all the ingredients mentioned under Koftas. Form round balls the size or a medium-sized lemon. Heat the oil in a frying pan. When it smokes, deep fry the balls a few at a time. Drain when golden brown. Set aside.

Next prepare the gravy. Heat the oil. Add the ground paste. Fry on a low flame for about 3 minutes, stirring often. Add the cashewnut powder and stir for a m inute. Add the turmeric powder, chilli powder and tomatoes. Cook uncovered on a low flame for about 3 minutes, stirring often. Add the water and salt. Bring to a boil. Cook covered on a low flame for 3 minutes. Add the curd, cream and garam masala. Cook uncovered on a low flame for 3 minutes, stirring continuously

Just before serving, reheat the gravy, add the koftas and bring to a quick boil. Garnish with coriander leaves.

Serve hot with chappatis, tandoori rotis, naans or parathas.

SERVES : 4-6

Misi Methi Roti

Unleavened Mixed Flour and Fenugreek leaves

*The combination of two types of flour and fenugreek leaves
increases the nutritional value manifold besides enhancing the taste.
The main accompaniment to this dish is any vegetarian or
non-vegeterian preparation with or without gravy
(i.e. Kheema Mutter, Baigan Burtha, Malai Koftas).*

INGREDIENTS

2½ cups wheat flour
11¼ cups gram flour
½ tsp turmeric powder
½ tsp chilli powder (optional)
¼ tsp garam masala
½ tsp cummin seeds
1 cup fresh frenugreek leaves or
1 cup dry methi (Kasoori methi)
Water
Oil
Salt to taste

METHOD

Combine all the ingredients with the exception of oil and water. Add water little by little and prepare a slightly stiff dough. Add 1 teaspoon oil and knead the dough very well.

Divide the dough into 10 portions. Roll out each portion into a round roti about 7" in diameter. Cook each roti on a hot lightly greased griddle (tawa) on low flame till both sides are almost cooked. Add a little oil on both sides and cook on a high flame till both sides become slighly crisp and brown.

Serve hot during a regular meal accompanied by any preparation like Kheema Mutter, Baigan Bharta or Malai Koftas.

SERVES : 4-6

Navratna Korma
Multi-Coloured Vegetables

The combination of vegetables, fruit and cream lends this preparation great flavour, a rich and lovely consistency and the wee bit of sweet taste makes it stand apart from any other dish. Always ensure that the vegetables are firm and retain their colour so that the dish looks appetising. The main accompaniments to this dish are chappatis, tandoori rotis, naans or parathas.

INGREDIENTS

1½ cups small pieces mixed vegetables
(potatoes, green peas, carrots, French beans
and cauliflower)
12 squares cottage cheese, size ½" x ½"
16 squares pineapple, size ½" x ½"
2 tbsp oil
1 medium-sized onion ⎫
1 tbsp chopped ginger ⎬ Grind to a paste
1 tsp chopped garlic ⎪
2 green chillies ⎭
1 large tomato (immersed in hot water for
5 minutes, drained, peeled and chopped)
½ tsp turmeric powder
½ tsp chilli powder
1 cup fresh curd (beaten)
⅓ cup fresh cream (beaten)
½ cup water
¼ tsp garam masala
Salt to taste

For Garnishing
3 tbsp chopped coriander leaves
4 tinned cherries (optional)
1 tbsp grated cheese
1 tbsp medium pieces of cashewnuts
1 tbsp fried raisins

METHOD

Boil the vegetables in very little water to which salt is added. Remove from heat when the vegetables are almost cooked but not overcooked.

Heat the oil in a pan. Add the ground paste and fry on a low flame for about 5 minutes, stirring often. Add the tomato, turmeric powder and chilli powder. Cook uncovered for 5 minutes, stirring often. Add the curd and cream. Stir for 2 minutes. Add the water, salt and garam masala. Bring to a boil. Add the boiled vegetables, paneer and pineapple. Cook uncovered on a medium flame for about 5 minutes or until the vegetables are cooked. Garnish with coriander leaves, cherries, cheese, cashewnuts and raisins.

Serve hot with chappatis, tandoori rotis, naans

SERVES : 4-6

Navratna Rabri

Thickened Milk with Fruits

A dessert that will steal the show. It is beautiful, rich, sustaining, nutritious and most enjoyable.

INGREDIENTS

6 cups milk
4 tbsp sugar
6 strands saffron (optional)
2 crushed cardamoms
½ cup chopped mixed dry fruits (almonds, pistachio nuts, cashewnuts, raisins, dates, glacé cherries)
¾ cup chopped mixed fresh fruits (unpeeled apples with red skin, oranges, seedless grapes)

METHOD

Boil the milk. Cook uncovered on a low flame, stirring frequently. While stirring, move the cream that forms on the surface of the milk towards the sides of the pan. Remove 1 tablespoon hot milk, add the saffron, and rub the saffron between the fingers. Add this to the hot milk. When the milk reduces to ½ the original quantity, add the sugar, cardamom and the dry fruits. Stir and cook for 2 minutes. Remove from heat and cool at room temperature. Add the fresh fruits and mix well. Pour into a glass serving dish.

Place the glass dish in the refrigerator so that the Rabri gets chilled. Serve cold as a dessert.

SERVES : 4-6

Paneer Do Pyaza
Cottage Cheese with Onions

The onions, added at two stages, enhance the taste of this famous dish.
The main accompaniments to this dish are chappatis,
tandoori rotis, naans or parathas.

INGREDIENTS

2 tbsp oil
½ tsp cummin seeds
2 cloves
½" stick cinnamon
2 cardamoms
1 Bay leaf
2 medium-sized onions (peeled & chopped)
1 tbsp chopped ginger
1 tsp chopped garlic
1 tsp chopped green chillies
2 medium-sized tomatoes (immersed in hot water
for 5 minutes, drained, peeled & chopped)
½ tsp turmeric powder
½ tsp chilli powder
¼ tsp garam masala
½ cup fresh curd (beaten)
½ cup water
2 medium-sized onions
(peeled & cut into thin rings)
30 squares cottage cheese, size 1" x 1"
(fried brown)
½ cup chopped coriander leaves
Salt to taste

METHOD

Heat the oil. Add the cummin seeds, cloves, cinnamon, cardamoms and Bay leaf. Stir. Add the chopped onions, ginger, garlic and green chillies. Fry on a low flame for a few minutes, stirring often. When the onions become brown, add the tomatoes, turmeric powder, chilli powder and garam masala. Fry on a low flame for about 3 minutes. Add the curd. Fry on a low flame for about 3 minutes, stirring often. Add the water and salt. Bring to a boil, then add the onion rings and paneer. Cook covered on a low flame for about 5 minutes or until the paneer is quite soft. Garnish with coriander leaves.

Serve hot with chappatis, tandoori rotis, naans or parathas.

SERVES : 4-6

Pudina Paratha
Unleavened Mint Bread

The green colour makes these parathas look most inviting and unusual. Add oil to the paratha only when both sides are almost cooked and not beforehand, otherwise, the paratha may be undercooked in some places. In order that parathas, chappatis, and so on do not become soggy during storage, always place them on a napkin or piece of foil, placed within the container as well. Wrap them in this way and then cover the container as well. This also keeps the parathas warm for some time. The main accompaniment to this dish is any vegeterian or non-vegetarian preparation with or without gravy (eg. Palak Gosht, Dal Fry, Gobhi Musallam).

INGREDIENTS

4½ cups wheat flour
1 tbsp chopped green chillies (optional)
1 tbsp grated ginger (optional)
½ tsp cummin seeds
¼ tsp turmeric powder
1 cup chopped mint leaves
Water
Oil
Salt to taste

METHOD

Combine all the ingredients with the exception of the oil and water. Add the water little by little and prepare a slightly stiff dough. Add a teaspoon of oil and knead the dough very well.

Divide the dough into 10 portions. Roll out each portion into a round roti approximately 7" in diameter. Cook each roti on a hot lightly greased griddle (tawa) on a low flame till both sides are almost cooked. Add a little oil on both sides and cook on a high flame till both sides become slightly crisp and brown.

Serve hot during a regular meal accompanied with any preparation like Palak Gosht, Dal Fry, Gobhi Musallam and so on.

SERVES : 4-6

Punjabi Chhole
Punjabi Style White Gram

An easy method is used to prepare this popular and nutritious dish and that too, without a drop of oil indeed a boon to the weight conscious. To enhance the taste and visual appeal, special attention should be paid to garnishing with onion, green chilli, ginger, lemon, coriander leaves, tomato, and so on. The main accompaniments to this dish are puris, bhaturas or bread.

INGREDIENTS

1½ cups White gram (Kabuli chana)
A large pinch soda bi carbonate
1 tsp tea leaves (tie in a muslin cloth)

1 tsp chilli powder ⎤ Roast
¾ tsp garam masala ⎥ without oil and
2 tsp cummin seeds ⎥ grind to
2 tsp pomegranate seeds ⎦ powder

Thick tamarind juice to taste (optional)
Salt to taste

For Garnishing
2 green chillies (cut rougly)
2" piece ginger (peeled & cut into long thin pieces)
1 large onion (peeled & cut into thin round slices)
1 medium-sized tomato (cut into thin round slices)
¼ cup chopped coriander leaves
1 medium-sized lemon (cut into 8 pieces)

METHOD

Pick, wash and soak the white gram in water either overnight or for at least 8 hours.

Add the salt, soda bi carbonate and the tea pouch. Pressure cook the gram until soft, making sure it is not overcooked and mashed. Remove 2 tablespoons of the cooked gram, grind or mash well, and add it to the boiled gram. Cook uncovered on a low flame, stirring occasionally. Squeeze the tea bag, remove from the cooked gram and discard. When the gram is quite dry, add chilli powder, garam masala, cummin-pomegranate powder and tamarind juice. Mix well and pour into a serving dish. Arrange the chopped green chillies, ginger, onion, tomato, coriander leaves and lemon on top of the chanas. Serve hot with bhaturas or puris. Punjabi Chhole can also be served with bread, in which case, add more water to create some gravy.

This versatile dish can be served with a meal or as a snack or as a meal-in-a-dish.

SERVES : 4-6

Punjabi Samosa
Stuffed Pastry

A perennial favourite. It is a vegetarian delicacy and a favourite snack. However, different types of vegetarian or non-vegetarian fillings can be used. After frying, do not cover the samosas, as they will lose their crispiness. Should covering become necessary, use a wire mesh dome. The main accompaniment to this dish is coriander chutney.

INGREDIENTS

For The Filling
4 medium-sized potatoes
¼ cup shelled & boiled green peas
2 tbsp oil
A pinch of asafoetida
1 tbsp chopped green chillies
1 tsp cummin seeds
½ tsp turmeric powder
2 tsp chilli powder
2 tsp mango powder
½ tsp pepper
1 tsp garam masala
½ cup chopped coriander leaves
1 tbsp raisins
2 tbsp small pieces of cashewnuts
Salt to taste

For The Covering
3 cups refined flour (maida)
¼ tsp black cummin seeds
9 tbsp oil
½ cup water oil for frying
Salt to taste

METHOD

First prepare the filling. Boil, peel and chop the potatoes into very small pieces. Measure to make approximately 3 cups. Heat the oil. Add the asafoetida, green chillies and cummin seeds. Stir. Add the potatoes, green peas and the rest of the ingredients mentioned under filling. Fry on a low flame for about 5 minutes, stirring most of the time. Remove from heat and cool at room temperature. Divide this mixture into 18 portions and set aside.

Next prepare the covering. For this, combine the refined flour, black cummin seeds and salt. Add the oil and rub with fingers till the mixture resembles breadcrumbs. Add water a little at a time and prepare a stiff dough. Divide the dough into 9 portions. Roll out each portion into a very thin round disc about 7" in diameter. Cut each disc into 2 pieces through the centre, so that each portion looks like a semi-circle. Apply a little water on the edges of one semi-circle on one side only and form a cone. Stuff this cone with one portion of the filling. Apply a little water on the inside edges of the cone and press together to close the cone completely, making sure the filling does not come out from anywhere. Prepare the remaining cones in the same manner. These cones are called samosas.

Heat the oil in a frying pan. Deep fry the samosas, a few at a time, on a low flame. Drain with a perforated spatula when the samosas are crisp and golden brown all over.

Serve hot as a snack with coriander chutney or tomato ketchup.

SERVES : 4-6

Tandoori Paneer

Baked Cottage Cheese

A much sought after dish on all occasions. It is prepared in a simple and quick way. The main accompaniment to it is coriander chutney.

INGREDIENTS

24 pieces paneer, size 1" x ½"

For The Marinade
2 green chillies
1" piece ginger — Grind to a paste
6 cloves garlic
¾ cup curd
1 tsp coriander powder
¼ tsp garam masala
¼ tsp orange-red food colouring
¼ tsp cup oil
Salt to taste

Masala For Sprinkling On The Paneer Pieces After Baking
1 tsp roasted cummin powder
1 tsp chilli powder
1 tsp mango powder

For Garnishing
1 medium-sized onion
(peeled & cut into thin round slices)
1 medium-sized lemon (cut into 8 pieces)
6 green chillies (kept whole)
1" piece ginger (scraped & cut into long thin pieces)

METHOD

With the exception of the oil, combine all the ingredients mentioned under Marinade. Coat the paneer pieces with this mixture and set aside for 30 minutes.

Grease a baking tray. Arrange the paneer pieces in a single layer on it. Pour the marinade all over the paneer and sprinkle oil. Bake in a preheated oven at 450°F or about 10 to 12minutes.

Put the baked paneer pieces in a single layer on a serving dish. Sprinkle the masala all over the paneer pieces. Garnish with onion, lemon, green chilli and ginger pieces.

Serve immediately with chappatis, tandoori rotis, naans or with cocktails or as a snack or starter, accompanied by coriander chutney.

SERVES : 4-6

Rajasthani

Bikaneri Masala Papad
Spicy Papadam

An attractive and tempting accompaniment to a meal or as a cocktail snack which can be prepared in minutes even by a novice. To prevent the papads from becoming soggy, cool them throughly after deep frying and then store them in an airtight container. Further, be very swift in sprinkling the topping ingredients and that too just before serving and once this is done, hasten to serve the papads.

INGREDIENTS

6 big Bikaneri masala papads
Oil for frying

For Sprinkling on Top Of The Papads
2 medium-sized onions (peeled & chopped)
4 chopped green chillies
½ cup chopped coriander leaves
1½ tsp chilli powder
1 tsp mango powder

METHOD

The most important point to remember is that the green chilies and coriander leaves should be wiped with a clean napkin before chopping. If water clings to both ingredients, the papads will turn soggy.

Heat the oil in a frying pan. Fry the papads one at a time, making sure they do not become reddish and burnt. Drain, making sure the excess oil does not cling to the papads.

Arrange each papad immediately in six flat individual dishes. Sprinkle the onion, green chillies, coriander leaves, chilli powder and mango powder over the surface of each papad. Serve at once, so that the papads do not become soggy.

Should serving be delayed, fry and cool the papads for a few minutes and store in an airtight container. Sprinkle on the topping ingredients before serving.

Serve with cocktails or as an accompaniment to a meal.

SERVES : 4-6

Gatte Ka Saag
Curried Rolls

When vegetables are not handy, this mouth-watering and economical dish would be the right choice. To check whether the gattas are nicely cooked from within, pierce each with a knife which should come out clean. Very hard gattas are undesirable. The main accompaniments to this dish are chappatis.

INGREDIENTS

For The Gattas
1½ cups gram flour
2 tsp coriander powder
1 tsp chilli powder
¼ tsp garam masala
3 tbsp oil
3 tbsp fresh curd
A little water
Oil for frying
Salt to taste

For The Gravy
4 cups water
2 tbsp oil
1½ tsp cummin seeds
A pinch of asafoetida
2 green chillies (chopped)
1 cup sour curd (beaten with 1 cup water and
1 tsp gram flour)
½ tsp turmeric powder
½ tsp chilli powder
¼ tsp garam masala
¼ cup chopped coriander leaves
Salt to taste

METHOD

Combine the gram flour, soda bicarabonate, coriander powder, chilli powder, garam masala and salt. Add the oil and rub with fingers. Add the curd and mix. Add very little water and form a stiff dough. Divide the dough into 4 portions. From each portion, prepare a ½" thick approximately 4" long roll. Boil the 4 cups water mentioned under Gravy. Add the 4 rolls making sure they are below the water level. Cook uncovered on a high flame for about 10 minutes or until the rolls are cooked. Remove from the fire. Drain the rolls and cool at room temperature. Do not discard the water in which the gattas were boiled as this can be used in the gravy.

When the gattas turn cold, cut them into ½" long pieces. Heat the oil in a frying pan. Deep fry all the pieces. Drain when golden brown. Set aside.

Heat the oil. Add the cummin seeds, asafoetida and green chillies. Stir. Add the curd, water and gram flour mixture, turmeric powder, chilli powder and garam masala. Bring to a boil, stirring continuously. Add the water in which the gattas were boiled and some salt. Bring to a boil. Cook uncovered on a medium flame for about 3 minutes. Add the gattas. Cook covered on a low flame for about 7 minutes. Garnish with fresh coriander leaves.

Serve hot with chappatis.

SERVES : 4-6

Ghaat Karbe

Broken Maize Porridge

An unusual, nutritious, palatable, quick and easy breakfast dish.
The main accompaniment to this dish is either fresh curd,
salted buttermilk or hot milk.

INGREDIENTS

3 tbsp melted ghee
1 cup coarse variety of broken maize (makai)
8 cups water
4 peppercorns (optional)
½ tsp pepper
Salt to taste

Accompaniments
Fresh curd or milk or salted buttermilk

METHOD

To prepare the broken maize, roast it on a hot tawa without ghee, for about 3 minutes, stirring often. Remove from heat. Dry grind in a mixer until coarse pieces of maize are visible.

Heat the ghee. Add the broken maize. Fry on a low flame, stirring continuously, for about 5 minutes or until the broken maize becomes golden brown. Add the water and peppercorns. Stir well. Pressure cook the broken maize till it becomes soft (i.e. after 1 whistle, pressure cook on a low flame for about 15 minutes).

When the pressure cooker is opened, add salt and pepper. Cook uncovered on a low flame for about 2 minutes.

Serve hot or at room temperature, for breakfast, with either fresh curd, salted buttermilk or hot milk, which should be combined with the cooked mixture a little at a time while eating.

SERVES : 4-6

Jaipuri Sabzi
Mixed Vegetables

These crunchy looking vegetables retain all their nutrients while combining to form a memorable dish. The main accompaniments to this dish are chappatis, parathas, tandoori rotis or naans.

INGREDIENTS

5 tbsp oil
2 medium-sized capsicums
(seeds removed & each cut into 8 pieces)
4 spring onions or
4 very small onions (peeled & cut
into 4 pieces each)
¼ cup medium-sized pieces of cauliflower
¼ cup 1" long pieces of French beans
¼ cup squares of carrot
1 tsp chopped ginger
4 green chillies (each slit into 2
through the centre)
4 medium-sized tomatoes (immersed in hot
water for 5 minutes, drained,
peeled & chopped)
¼ cup water
½ tsp turmeric powder
½ tsp chilli powder
½ tsp garam masala
2 tbsp chopped coriander leaves
Salt to taste

METHOD

Heat 4 tablespoons oil. Add the capsicum pieces. Fry on a high flame for a minute, stirring continuously. Drain all the vegetables together and set aside separately. Add the onion and fry in the same manner briefly. Then add the cauliflower, French beans, carrot and salt. Fry all the vegetables together in the same manner for 2 minutes. Remove the vegetables from the pan and set aside.

Add the remaining tablespoon of oil into the same pan. Add the ginger and green chillies. Fry briefly on a high flame. Add the tomatoes. Cook on a high flame for 2 minutes, stirring continuously. Add the water, turmeric powder, chilli powder, garam masala and salt. Bring to a boil. Add all the fried vegetables, except the capsicum.

Cook covered on a low flame for about 3 minutes. Add the capsicum. Cook uncovered on a high flame for a minute. Garnish with coriander leaves.

Serve hot with either chappatis, parathas, tandoori rotis or naans.

SERVES : 4-6

Marwari Curry

Rich Curd Curry

This slightly sour curry tastes superb due to the proper blending of various spices with the small pakories made in the traditional Rajasthani manner. It can be served at parties as well as for Sunday lunch. The main accompaniment to this dish is rice or chappatis.

INGREDIENTS

For The Curry
1 cup sour curd
¾ cup gram flour
7 cups water
¾ tsp turmeric powder
¾ tsp chilli powder
½ tsp garam masala
Salt to taste

For The Vaghar
6 tbsp oil
2 medium-sized onions (peeled & chopped)
2 green chillies (chopped)
A pinch of asafoetida
2 Kashmiri chillies
¾ tbsp cummin seeds

For The Garnishing
½ cup chopped coriander leaves

For The Pakories
1 cup gram flour
¼ cup chopped mint leaves chopped
1 tbsp chopped coriander leaves
1 green chilli (chopped)
1 tsp chilli powder
¼ tsp turmeric powder
1 tsp coriander powder
Very little water
Oil for frying
Salt to taste

METHOD

First prepare the pakories. Combine all the ingredients mentioned under Pakories, except for the water and oil. Add 2 tablespoons oil and rub with your fingers. Add very little water and prepare a stiff dough. Make marble-sized balls from the dough. Heat oil and deep fry the balls over a low flame. Drain when light brown and set aside.

Next prepare the curry. Combine the curd and gram flour. Add 1 cup water and rub with fingers to remove lumps. Add the remaining 6 cups of water and churn so that there are absolutely no lumps. Pour this mixture into a thick pan and place the pan on the flame. Add the turmeric powder, chilli powder, garam masala and salt. Bring to a boil, stirring almost continuously. Reduce the flame and cook uncovered for about 10 minutes, stirring occasionally. Add the pakories. Cook partly covered on a low flame for about 5 minutes. Just before serving, add the vaghar. For this, heat 4 tablespoons oil and fry the onion and green chillies on a low flame, stirring often, until the onion becomes light brown. Add this to the curry and mix. Heat the remaining 2 tablespoons oil separately and add the asafoetida, Kashmiri chillies and cummin seeds. When the cummin seeds become red, add these to the curry. Garnish with coriander leaves.

Serve hot with rice or chappatis.

SERVES : 4-6

Marwari Tekadiya

Spicy Unleavened Bread

These are unusual and delicious parathas stuffed with aromatic spices. These parathas are so delectable that they can also be eaten without any accompaniment or just with pickle or curd. The main accompaniment to this dish is any vegetable preparation with or without gravy.

INGREDIENTS

For The Tekadiyas
3 cups wheat flour
Water
Salt to taste

For The Stuffing
1 tsp cummin seeds
2 tsp coarsely crushed peppercorns
3 tsp chilli powder
2 tsp roasted cummin powder
2 tsp mango powder
2 tsp garam masala

METHOD

Combine all the stuffing ingredients. Divide into 8 portions and set aside.

Combine the wheat flour and salt. Add water a little at a time and prepare a pliable dough (i.e. slightly stiffer than chappati dough). Add 1 tablespoon oil and knead the dough very well. Divide the dough into 8 portions.

Roll out one portion of dough to a diameter of 3". Place a portion of the stuffing in the centre, bring the edges together, making sure that the stuffing is completely enclosed. Roll out again with a light touch to a diameter of 7". Roast on a hot griddle (tawa), on a low flame till both sides are almost cooked. Add a little oil on both sides of the paratha and cook on a high flame until brown on both sides. Prepare the remaining parathas in the same manner.

Serve hot with any vegetable preparation.

SERVES : 4-6

Mung Dal Seera
Split Yellow Lentil Sweet

*A favourite dessert to be served hot in the chilly winter months.
In order to prevent dal from sticking to the pan,
always add it to hot ghee.*

INGREDIENTS

2 cups yellow mung dal
1 cup melted ghee
½ cup water
3 cups milk
3 cups sugar
6 crushed cardamoms
6 almonds (blanched & cut into
long thin pieces)
8 pistachio nuts(blanched & cut into
long thin pieces)
¾ cup solidified milk (mawa)
¼ tsp kewra essence
Silver leaf (vark)

METHOD

Pick, wash and soak the dal for about 4 hours. Drain and grind to a fine paste.

Heat the ghee in a thick-bottomed pan. Add the ground paste and fry on a low flame using a flat spatula, stirring frequently, until the dal becomes golden. Remember that the dal should never be added to cold ghee, as this will result in the dal sticking to the pan. When the dal becomes golden, add the water and stir continuously for 2 minutes. Then add the milk. Bring to a boil, stirring often. Cook uncovered on a low flame, stirring often, until the milk is nearly absorbed by the dal.

Add the sugar, cardamom, ½ the almonds and pistachio nuts and all the mawa. Cook on a low flame for a few minutes, stirring continuously, until the seera becomes quite dry. Add the kewra essence and mix well. Remove from heat and arrange on a serving dish. Garnish with the remaining almonds and pistachio nuts and the silver leaf.

Serve very hot as a dessert.

SERVES : 4-6

Ram Khichri
Pulao with Spicy Rolls

*This unique pulao is so tasty that it is not only suitable
for all occasions but is also a meal-in-a-dish.*

INGREDIENTS

For The Spicy Rolls (Gattas)
1 cup gram flour
A pinch of soda bi carbonate
2 tsp coriander powder
1 tsp chilli powder
1 tsp garam masala
2 tbsp oil
2 tsp fresh curd
Very little water for mixing
Oil for frying
3 cups water for boiling the gattas in
Salt to taste

For The Rice
1½ cups long-grained rice
3 tbsp melted ghee
3 cloves
½" stick cinnamon
3 cardamoms
5½ tsp turmeric powder
3 cups water
Salt to taste
1 tbsp raisins (fried)
1 tbsp small pieces of cashewnuts (fried)

METHOD

Combine the gram flour, soda bi carbonate, coriander powder, chilli powder, garam masala and salt. Add the oil and rub with fingers. Add the curd and mix. Add very little water and form a stiff dough. Divide the dough into 3 portions. From each portion, prepare a ½" thick 4" long roll.

Boil the water. Add 3 gatta rolls. Cook uncovered on a high flame for about 10 minutes or until cooked. Remove from heat. Drain the rolls and cool at room temperature. With a sharp knife, make ½" long pieces from all the rolls. Heat the oil in a frying pan and deep fry all the chopped pieces. Drain when light brown. Set aside.

Heat the ghee in a thick-bottomed pan. Add the cloves, cinnamon and cardamoms. Stir. Add the drained rice and fry for 2 minutes. Add the turmeric powder, and salt. Stir and bring to a boil. Cook covered on a low flame for a few minutes until the rice is half cooked. Add the gattas. Cook covered on a low flame for a few minutes until the rice is cooked, stirring twice in-between. Garnish with raisins and cashewnuts.

Serve hot with a regular meal or as a meal-in-a-dish.

SERVES : 4-6

Thuli

Broken Wheat Porridge

A highly nutritious and quick breakfast dish. The main accompaniment to it is fresh curd or hot milk.

INGREDIENTS

3 tbsp melted ghee
1 cup coarse variety broken wheat (dalia),
available readymade
5 cups water
6 peppercorns
2 crushed cardamoms
A big pinch of salt

Accompaniments
Fresh curd or hot milk with or without sugar

METHOD

Heat the ghee. Add the broken wheat. Fry on a low flame, stirring continuously, for about 5 minutes or until the broken wheat becomes golden brown. Add the water and peppercorns. Stir well. Pressure cook the broken wheat till it becomes soft (i.e. after 1 whistle, pressure cook on a low flame for about 10 minutes).

When the pressure cooker is opened, add the salt and cardamoms. Cook uncovered on a low flame for about 3 minutes, stirring once in-between.

Serve hot or at room temperature as a breakfast dish, with fresh curd or hot milk, with or without sugar. The curd or milk should be mixed with the cooked broken wheat gradually before eating.

SERVES : 4-6

Sindhi

Fotan Varo Teevan

Mutton with Cardamom

*Here, mutton is cooked with cardamom, which gives this dish a distinctive flavour. Although a favourite with most people, this dish is often served to women immediately after childbirth, as it does not contain onions which many people believe women should not consume at this stage.
For this purpose, the green chillies, ginger and chilli powder may be deleted, if desired. In order to obtain maximum flavour from the cardamoms, crush the seeds and pods before using them. The main accompaniments to this dish are chappatis.*

INGREDIENTS

500 gms mutton
10 cardamoms
4 green chillies
1" piece ginger
4 tbsp oil
1 tsp pepper powder
½ tsp chilli powder
2 cups water
½ cup chopped coriander leaves
Salt to taste

METHOD

Cut the mutton into medium-sized pieces and wash well. Set aside.

Crush the cardamom seeds and pods into a coarse powder. Slit each green chilli into 2 pieces through the centre. Scrape and cut the ginger into long thin pieces.

Heat the oil and add the cardamom powder, green chillies and ginger. Fry for a minute on a low flame, stirring continuously. Add the mutton and fry on a medium flame for about 5-7 minutes, stirring almost continuously. Add the pepper powder, chilli powder and fry for a minute. Add the water and salt. Pressure cook the mutton until tender (i.e. after 1 whistle, pressure cook on a low flame for about 20 minutes). When the pressure cooker is opened, cook partly covered on a low flame for about 2 minutes. Garnish with coriander leaves.

Serve hot with chappatis.

SERVES : 4-6

Rasvari Machhi
Fish Curry

A simple and straightforward method is used to prepare this mouth-watering dish. The whole garlic cloves not only look stunning while floating in the gravy but also taste wonderful, thereby making this dish a real treat. Do not make the mistake of chopping or crushing the garlic, as the presence of full cloves of garlic is a must. The main accompaniment to this dish is chappatis or rice.

INGREDIENTS

10 medium-sized pieces of pomfret
or surmai fish
6 tbsp oil
6 cardamoms
24 cloves garlic (peeled & kept whole)
6 green chillies ⎤ Mix
½ cup coriander leaves ⎟ together
5 large red tomatoes ⎬ & grind
1" piece ginger ⎦ to a
⎦ paste)
1 tsp chilli powder
½ tsp turmeric powder
3 tsp coriander powder
2¼ cups water
Salt to taste

METHOD

Wash the fish, rub salt all over them and set aside for 30 minutes. After 30 minutes, wash again.

Heat the oil. Add the cardamom seeds and skins. Stir. Add the whole garlic cloves. Stir. Add the ground masala paste. Fry on a low flame for a few minutes, stirring often, until there is no water left and oil floats on top. Add the chilli powder, turmeric powder, coriander powder and salt. Stir. Add the fish. Cook covered on a low flame for 5 minutes.

Turn over the fish pieces and add the water. Bring to a boil. Cook covered on a low flame for about 5 minutes or until the fish is done.

Serve hot with rice or chappatis.

Seyal Murgi

Steamed Chicken with Onions

*Chicken is cooked with spices in the traditional Sindhi manner,
which gives it a distinctive taste. This dish will be at its best
if the gravy is negligible and the chicken is not overcooked.
The main accompaniments to this dish are chappatis.*

INGREDIENTS

600 gms chicken
4 tbsp oil
3 medium-sized onions (peeled & chopped)
3 medium-sized tomatoes (chopped)
4 green chillies (chopped)
½" piece ginger (chopped)
8 cloves garlic (chopped)
½ cup fresh curd (beaten)
1 tsp coriander powder
1 tsp chilli powder

METHOD

Clean and cut the chicken into medium-sized pieces. Wash well.

Heat the oil and fry the onion on a low flame, stirring often. When the onion starts changing colour, add the green chillies, ginger and garlic. Fry for a minute. Add the tomatoes and cook covered for about 3 minutes. Mash the tomatoes lightly. Add the curd, coriander powder, chilli powder, turmeric powder, salt and the chicken pieces. Fry over a medium flame for about 5 minutes, stirring often. Pressure cook the chicken until done (i.e. after 1 whistle, pressure cook on a low flame for about 8 minutes). When the pressure cooker is opened, cook uncovered on a low flame for about 5 minutes or until no liquid is left. Add the garam masala and coriander leaves.

Serve hot with chappatis or bread.

SERVES : 4-6

Chana Dal Pattis

Bengal Gram Patties

The chana dal stuffing makes this dish nutritious and attractive and provides a good variation from the routine stuffings. The main accompaniment to this dish is coriander chutney.

INGREIDENTS

For The Stuffing
½ cup Bengal gram
¼ tsp turmeric powder
½ tsp chilli powder
½ tsp mango powder
½ tsp garam masala
½ tsp pepper
2 tbsp raisins
2 tbsp cashewnut pieces
Salt to taste

For The Covering
6 medium-sized potatoes
(boiled, peeled & mashed)
4 slices bread(soaked in water
drained & squeezed)
Oil for frying
Salt to taste

METHOD

Pick and wash the dal. Add the turmeric powder, salt and the least amount of water required to cook the dal. Pressure cook until the dal is soft but not overcooked (i.e. each grain of dal should be visible). Drain out excess water from the dal. Add the rest of the ingredients mentioned under stuffing and mix well. Divide this mixture into 12 portions and set aside.

Next prepare the covering. For this, combine the potatoes, bread and salt. Knead well to prepare a smooth mixture. Divide this mixture into 24 portions. Take 2 portions of the potato mixture and flatten each separately, using a little oil to do this. Place one flattened portion of the potato mixture on your palm, put 1 portion of the dal mixture on top of it and cover with the second flattened portion of the potato mixture. Smoothen and seal the edges using a few drops of oil, so that the pattie looks neat and the dal does not come out from anywhere. Prepare the remaining patties in the same manner.

Heat a little oil on a tawa or a flat non-sick pan. Shallow fry the patties a few at a time. Drain when golden brown.

Serve hot as a snack or starter, accompanied by coriander chutney.

*For best results, use freshly boiled potatoes. Further, remove the potatoes from the water as soon as they are cooked.

SERVES : 4-6

Dal Pakwan

Lentils with Crisp Unleavened Bread

A favourite and extremely popular Sunday breakfast delicacy in Sindhi homes. The dal is prepared without a drop of oil. In order to obtain unpuffed crispy pakwans, always prick them before frying. The main accompaniment to this dish is coriander chutney.

INGREDIENTS

For The Pakwans
1½ cups refined flour (maida)
Oil for deep frying
¼ tsp salt

For The Dal
1½ cups Bengal gram
½ tsp turmeric powder
½ tsp chilli powder
½ tsp mango powder
½ tsp garam masala
4 green chillies (cut into big pieces)
2 tsp chopped coriander leaves
Salt to taste

For the Accompaniments
¾ cup coriander chutney
¾ cup chopped onion

METHOD

First prepare the pakwans. For this, sieve the flour. Add the salt and mix well. Add water a little at a time and prepare a stiff dough. Make small balls from the dough and roll out each ball into a thin round disc about 6" in diameter. Prick with a fork or knife here and threre very lightly. This will prevent the pakwans from puffing up while frying. Heat the oil in a frying pan. Deep fry all the pakwans one by one, pressing downwards while frying on a low flame. Drain with a perforated spatula when both sides of each pakwan are crisp and brown. Set aside uncovered or cool thoroughly and place in an airtight container until required.

Next prepare the dal. Pick, wash and soak the dal in water for about 30 minutes. Add the turmeric powder and salt. Pressure cook until the dal is soft but not overcooked (i.e. each grain of dal should be visible). Add the remaining ingredients mentioned under Dal, except the coriander leaves. Cook uncovered on a low flame for about 5 minutes or until the dal achieves a medium thickness. While cooking, stir the dal a few times, but make absolutely sure that the individual dal grains are still visible. Garnish with fresh coriander leaves.

Serve piping hot dal with the prepared pakwans for breakfast or as a meal-in-a-dish. Serve the accompaniments in separate bowls, so that they can be added to the dal as required, just before eating.

Dalpaati
Unleavened Lentil Bread

*These parathas are so delicious when served hot or cold, that the taste
lingers in the mouth and mind as well! Cold dalpaatis (dal parathas) are
served the day after preparation to celebrate a religious ritual called Thadri,
in honour of Sitla Maata. The stuffed dalpaatis should always be rolled out
with a light pressure, so that the stuffing does not come out. Further, the
moisture from hot cooked parathas invariably makes them soggy on
storage. To prevent this, always wrap the parathas in a thin napkin or a
piece of foil. This way, they will also remain hot for a longer time.
If you want to preserve cold parathas for the next day, cool them
thoroughly in a broad tray and then wrap them in a napkin or piece
of foil. If parathas are wrapped when they are hot and preserved for
a long time, they are likely to develop a bad odour. The main
accompaniments to this dish are fresh curd, pickle, sai bhaji
or any other vegetable preparation.*

INGREDIENTS

For The Filling
1½ cups yellow mung dal
3 cups water
1 tsp oil
¼ tsp turmeric powder
2 tsp chilli powder
1 tsp mango powder
1 tsp garam masala
Salt to taste

For The Dough
4 cups wheat flour
Oil
Salt to taste

METHOD

Pick, wash and soak the dal in 3 cups of water for
30 minutes. Heat the oil in a pan. Add the dal
along with the water, turmeric powder and salt.
Bring to a boil. Cook covered on a low flame for
about 15 minutes, stirring a few times, or until the
dal is soft but not overcooked. Each grain of dal
should be visible and there should be absolutely
no water. Remove from heat and cool the dal. Add
the remaining ingredients mentioned under
Filling. Mix well and divide this mixture into 10
portions. Set aside.

Next prepare the dough. Combine the flour
and salt. Mix. Add water a little at a time and
prepare a dough very slightly stiffer than chappati

SERVES : 4-6

dough. Divide this dough into 10 portions. Roll out 1 portion of the dough to a diameter of about 3½". Spread ¼ teaspoon oil on it. Place a portion of the dal mixture in the centre, bring the edges together, close and form a ball. Roll out this ball very carefully with a light pressure into a round paratha about 7" in diameter, makng sure that the filling does not come out. Cook the paratha on a hot lighly greased tawa on a low flame till both sides are almost cooked. Add a little oil on both sides and cook on a high flame till both sides become brown. Prepare the remaining parathas in the same manner. Serve hot with fresh curd, pickle or any other vegetable curry as a breakfast dish or during a regular meal.

Very often, cold dalpaatis (preserved at room temperature) are served the next day with curd, pickle or fried brinjals (also prepared the previous day). This is done to observe a religious ritual called *Thadri* in honour of Sitla Maata. It is believed that on this occasion, cold dalpaatis should not be eaten along with any food that may be prepared on that day.

Dhaaran ji Chutney
Coriander Chutney

This chutney is not only nutritious and versatile but also very easy to prepare. Moreover, it can be preserved in the refrigerator for at least a week and hence comes in handy as an accompaniment to various snacks. The main accompaniment to this dish is any fried snack such as Chana Dal Pattis, Sana Pakoras and so on.

INGREDIENTS

6 cups chopped coriander leaves
1 cup chopped mint leaves
10 green chillies (chopped)
1 tsp cummin seeds
1 tbsp chopped ginger(optional)
Juice of a medium-sized lemon
Salt to taste

METHOD

Wash the coriander and mint leaves in plenty of water.

Combine all the given ingredients, with the exception of the lemon juice, and grind to a fine paste.

Add the lemon juice to the ground paste and mix well.

Store this chutney in a covered container. It can be preserved for at least a week.

Serve this chutney with snacks like kababs, samosas, pattis, pakoras and so on, or as an accompaniment to a meal.

SERVES : 4-6

Khoyo
Rich Winter Sweet

This dessert/sweet is a delicacy amongst Sindhis, who prepare it in winter. The ingredients are available at typical Sindhi provision stores known as Ochi Pasari. This dessert/sweet is usually prepared in large quantities and stored for some days. It can be preserved outside the refrigerator for about 4 days and for about 15-20 days in the refrigerator. It can be easily removed from the refrigerator, reheated and served hot. This dish will be relished only if it is served piping hot.

INGREDIENTS

12 cups (2 litres) milk
1 cup (125 gms) dry dates
¾ cup(75 gms) poppy seeds
½ cup (50 gms) thick husk of coriander seeds
6 strands saffron
¾ tbsp crushed black cardamom seeds
1 tsp crushed green cardamom
¾ cup melted ghee
1½ cups sugar
½ tbsp mace & nutmeg powder
¾ tbsp muhsafai (white powder) optional
1 tsp muhlalai (orange/red food colouring)
½ cup small pieces of cashewnuts
¼ cup almonds(blanched & chopped into long thin pieces)
2 tbsp pistachio nuts (blanched & sliced)

METHOD

Pick the poppy seeds and the husk of coriander seeds separately, ensuring that there are absolutely no stones. Wash, drain and add a cup of cold milk each to the poppy seeds and the husk of coriander seeds and grind each item separately in a mixer, coarsely. Excessive grinding is not at all desirable. Set aside. Place dry dates on a newspaper and smash with a hammer. Break the dates into 4-6 pieces each and discard the seeds. Wash the dates and set aside.

Boil the remaining 10 cups milk. Remove a tablespoon of hot milk, add to the saffron, rub with your fingers and set aside. Add the ground poppy seeds and the coriander seeds husk mixture to the milk together with the washed dates. Cook uncovered on a low flame, stirring occasionally, for about 2 hours. Add the tablespoon of saffron milk, both the cardamoms and ½ cup ghee. Stir. Add ¾ cup sugar and cook for 3 minutes, stirring continuously. Add the mace and nutmeg powder, muhsafai (this prevents flatulence), and the remaining ¾ cup sugar.

Cook uncovered on a low flame, stirring continuously for about 10 minutes or until almost dry. Add muhsafai (colouring) mixed with a tablespoon of water, remaining ¼ cup ghee, the cashewnuts, almonds and pistachio nuts. Stir continuously for about 5 minutes. Remove from heat and serve hot. Alternatively, cool thoroughly at room temperature and store in a refrigerator , duly covered and serve when needed. Remove the required quantity from the refrigerator with a dry spoon, reheat on a low flame and serve hot.

SERVES : 4-6

Koki

Spicy Unleavened Bread

Delicious and distinctive, this breakfast dish is a must and has created a place for itself in Sindhi homes. It is generally served with fresh curd or pickle. In order for the Koki not to break while being cooked on the tawa, prevent the edges getting cracked by closing them up constantly by hand. The main accompaniment to this dish is fresh curd or pickle.

INGREDIENTS

4½ cups wheat flour
½ cup chopped mint leaves
¼ cup chopped coriander leaves
4 tsp green chillies (chopped)
1 medium-sized onion (peeled & chopped) - optional
½ cup melted ghee or oil
A little water
Oil or ghee for frying
Salt to taste

METHOD

Mix the flour, mint leaves, coriander leaves, green chillies, onion and salt. Add the ghee or oil and rub with your fingers till the mixture resembles breadcrumbs. Add very little water and prepare a smooth stiff dough, so that it can be rolled out without the help of dry flour.

Divide the dough into 6 equal portions. Roll out each portion into a $1/8$" thick round disc. Prick here and there with a fork on both sides. Cook one by one on a tawa on a low flame till both sides turn light brown. Add a little ghee or oil on both sides of each disc and cook over a medium flame until both sides become golden brown.

Serve hot with fresh curd or pickle, as a breakfast dish.

SERVES : 4-6

Lolo
Sweet Stiff Bread

So rich and so delicious that the taste lingers. Can be served hot or cold. Cold lolas are also served on the day following preparation, to celebrate a religious ritual called Thadri. *The main accompaniment to this dish is fresh curd or pickle.*

INGREDIENTS

6 cups wheat flour
1½ cups melted ghee
1½ cups powdered sugar mixed with
½ cup water
12 tbsp oil or melted ghee for frying
6 tbsp wheat flour for sprinkling while rolling

METHOD

Add 1½ cups melted ghee a little at a time, to the 6 cups flour. Then add the sugar and water mixture and prepare a stiff dough. Knead the dough well and divide into 6 equal portions. Make smooth round balls closing the edges, so that they do not crack.

Sprinkle a tablespoon of wheat flour on a rolling board and roll one ball very carefully to make a ¼" thick round disc, approximately 5" in diameter. Roll the remaining balls in the same manner. Place all the rolled discs on a dry napkin in a single layer.

Heat a tawa and spread a little oil or ghee on it. Put 1 rolled disc (lolo) on it. Cook on a low flame moving the lolo carefully with your hand or with a flat spatula. Do not lift the lolo as it will break. When one side is light brown, slide it onto a flat plate and put the uncooked side on the tawa. Cook this side till light brown. Put a tablespoon of oil or melted ghee on the top and at the edges of each side of the lolo and cook until golden brown. Prepare the remaining discs in the same manner.

Serve hot with fresh curd or any pickle.

The prepared lolos can be preserved in a covered container outside the refrigerator for 2 days and inside the refrigerator for about 5 days. They can also be eaten cold.

Cold lolas are served on the day following prepration to observe a religious ritual called *Thadri* in honour of Sitla Maata and it is believed they should not be eaten with any food prepared on that day.

SERVES : 4-6

Mohanthal

Gram Flour Sweet

This popular sweet is not only economical but quick and easy to prepare. It is served during Diwali and especially at wedding lunches. For best results, add the hot syrup to the cold fried gram flour mixture and stir without cooking till the mixture becomes dry.

INGREDIENTS

$^2/_3$ cup melted ghee
1 cup gram flour (besan)
¼ cup fine semolina (soji)
$^1/_3$ cup milk

For The Syrup
$^2/_3$ cup sugar
$^1/_3$ cup water
4 crushed cardamoms

For The Top
10 almonds (cut into long thin pieces with skin)

METHOD

Heat the ghee in a heavy pan or a non-stick pan. Add the gram flour and semolina. Fry on a low flame, stirring continuously for about 5 minutes or until the mixture becomes golden brown. Add the milk and stir briskly till the milk evaporates. Remove from heat and set aside.

Next prepare the syrup. Combine the sugar and water in a pan. Cook on high heat and stir until the sugar dissolves. Cook uncovered on a low flame, stirring often, for about 5 minutes, so that the syrup becomes sticky. Add the cardamoms and remove from heat. Add this syrup to the fried gram flour. Without cooking, stir continuously for about 3 minutes so that the mixture becomes slightly cold and dry. Spread the mixture in a flat greased tray or thali to a thickness of ½" and level the surface. Sprinkle and lightly press in the chopped almonds on top. Mark into 1"x1" squares or larger squares or diamond shapes. Set aside for about 30 minutes to dry. Remove the pieces carefully with a flat spatula and store in an airtight container.

SERVES : 4-6

Sai Bhaji
Spinach

A simple and straightforward method is used to prepare this famous and highly nutritious dish, which is generally served with khichri and curd. A thorough churning of all the ingredients in order to obtain a smooth mixture is very important, as the right appearance and taste depends on this. The main accompaniment to this dish is either chappatis, puris or khichri.

INGREDIENTS

1 medium-sized bunch spinach
1 very small bunch dill (suva) bhaji
1 very small bunch khata bhaji
6 sprigs fenugreek (methi) bhaji
½ cup small cubes of bottle gourd
½ cup small pieces of brinjal
½ cup small pieces of carrot
¼ cup small pieces of cluster beans (gavar)
½ cup small pieces of tomato
½" piece ginger (scraped & chopped)
2 medium-sized green chillies (chopped)
¹/₃ cup Bengal gram (chana dal)
¼ cup split green gram (green mung dal)
1½ cups water
½ tsp turmeric powder
½ cup chilli powder
Salt to taste

For The Vaghar
2 tbsp oil
A pinch of asafoétida
½ tsp cummin seeds
2 medium green chillies (chopped)

METHOD

Wash the dals and soak them together in a cup of water for about 15 minutes.

Clean and chop the spinach, suva, khata and methi bhajis. Wash in plenty of water to get rid of the mud that usually clings to such vegetables. Combine the bottle gourd, brinjal, carrot and cluster beans. Wash in water and drain.

Pressure cook the washed green leafy vegetables as well as the other vegetables. Then put the dals together with the water in which they were soaked. Add the tomato, ginger, green chillies, remaining ½ cup water, turmeric powder and salt. Pressure cook the vegetables till soft (i.e. after 1 whistle, pressure cook on a low flame for about 5 minutes). When done, beat the contents with an egg beater or wooden churner. Cook uncovered on a low flame for about 5 minutes, stirring twice.

Heat the oil separately in a tiny pan. Add the asafoetida, cummin seeds and green chillies. When the cummin seeds become light brown, add the contents to the mashed spinach. Remove the spinach from the flame.

Serve hot with chappatis, puris and/or khichri.

Sai Bhaji can easily be served without a drop of oil. To do this, omit the oil and roast the remaining vagar ingredients in a non-stick pan.

SERVES : 4-6

Sana Pakora

Small Fried Balls

A delicious, extremely popular and versatile dish. An ideal choice for entertaining unexpected guests. The main accompaniment to this dish is either coriander chutney, puris or bread.

INGREDIENTS

1¼ cups gram flour
A pinch of soda bi carbonate
¼ cup finely chopped potatoes
¼ cup finely chopped onion
¼ cup finely chopped bottle gourd
¼ cup finely chopped brinjal
2 tbsp chopped raw mango (optional)
½ tsp pomegranate seeds (optional)
1½ tsp coriander seeds
1 tsp chopped green chillies
1 tbsp chopped mint leaves
½ cup chopped coriander leaves
1 tsp chilli powder
A little water to mix
Oil for frying
Salt to taste

METHOD

Mix the gram flour and soda bi carbonate. Add the remaining ingredients to this mixture with the exception of the water and oil. Add water a little at a time and prepare a smooth batter of thick consistency.

Heat oil in a frying pan till it starts smoking. Drop lumps of the prepared batter (either by hand or with a tablespoon) into the oil. Fry over a medium flame till the batter turns light brown. Drain, cool and break each pakora into 2 or 3 pieces. At the time of serving, re-fry the pakoras till crisp and golden in colour.

Serve hot with coriander chutney and/or tomato sauce. Sana Pakora is suitable as a side dish to a meal, a tea-time snack or with cocktails. Sana Pakora also makes an excellent light meal. For a light meal, the following combinations are ideal:

1) Sana Pakora, puris, coriander chutney
2) Sana Pakora, sliced/loaf bread, sliced onion, coriander chutney

SERVES : 4-6

Seyal Maani

Soft Spicy Unleavened Bread

An excellent dish to cut down on wastage of left over chappatis.
It tastes so good that many people prepare this dish even from
freshly made chappatis.

INGREDIENTS

10 leftover chappatis
20 tbsp coriander chutney
4 tbsp oil
A pinch of asafoetida
½ tsp cummin seeds
2 medium-sized onions
(peeled & chopped)
1 tbsp ginger paste
1 tsp garlic paste
½ chilli powder
¼ tsp garam masala
¼ tsp mango powder
½ cup water
¼ cup chopped coriander leaves
Salt to taste

METHOD

Apply 1 tablespoon of coriander chutney on a chappati, spreading it all over one side only. Fold the chappati so that it looks like a semi-circle. Spread 1 tablespoon coriander chuteny on it. Fold the semi-circle so that it looks like a tringle. Repeat the same procedure with the remaining chappatis. Set aside.

Heat the oil in a board pan. Add the asafoetida and cummin seeds. Stir. Add the onions, ginger and garlic. Fry on a low flame for about 5 minutes, stirring often. Add the chilli powder, garam masala, mango powder and salt. Stir so that all the ingredients are well mixed. Arrange the chappati tringles on the onion mixture in a single layer. Add the water. Bring to a boil. Cook covered on a low flame for about 3 mintues. Turn over the triangles carefully. Cook covered on a low flame for about 3 minutes or until there is no water left. Garnish with coriander leaves.

Serve hot as a snack, for breakfast or as a meal-in-a-dish.

SERVES : 4-6

Sindhi Curry

Gram Flour, Lentil and Vegetable Curry

A mouth-watering concoction of various ingredients makes this dish a delicacy. It is generally served for Sunday lunch with rice. It is often served at wedding lunches. The main accompaniments to this dish are rice and sweet bundi.

INGREDIENTS

¾ cup toovar dal
2 tbsp gram flour
4 tbsp oil
½ tsp cummin seeds
½ tsp fenugreek seeds
½ tsp mustard seeds
A large pinch of asafoetida
20 cluster beans (gavar)
20 lady's fingers
16 drumstick pieces (3" long)
3 medium-sized potatoes
2 tsp large pieces of ginger
1 tsp large pieces of green chillies
30 curry leaves
8 cocums
¼ cup thick tamarind juice or as desired
¾ tsp turmeric powder
½ tsp chilli powder
9 cups water
¼ cup chopped coriander leaves
Salt to taste

METHOD

To prepare tamarind juice, wash and soak the tamarind in a little cold water for about 20 minutes. Rub with fingers and pass through a sieve. Wash and soak the cocum in ½ cup cold water just before you start preparing the curry.

Pick, wash and soak the toovar dal in 2 cups of water for about 20 minutes. Add salt and ¼ teaspoon turmeric powder and pressure cook till very soft. Mash thoroughly and set aside.

Heat the oil, add the gram flour and fry on a low flame, stirring continuously, until the gram flour becomes light brown. Add the cummin seeds, fenugreek seeds, mustard seeds and asafoetida. Continue frying the gram flour in the same manner until these seeds splutter. Add the chilli powder and stir quickly making sure the gram flour does not get burnt. Add the mashed dal, remaining 7 cups of water, the remaining ½ teaspoon turmeric powder and salt. Bring to a boil and cook uncovered on a low flame for about 5 minutes. Meanwhile, cut the vegetables. Wash the lady's fingers, top and tail, slit on one side through the centre, keeping them whole. Set aside.

Cut both ends of the cluster beans, keeping them whole. Wash the potatoes whole and cut each into 2 pieces, retaining the skin. Wash the cluster beans, drumsticks, potatoes and curry leaves together. Add these to the curry along with ginger and green chillies. Cook uncovered or partly covered (as the curry is likely to overflow) on a low flame, stirring occasionally, until the vegetables are half cooked. Add the lady's fingers and cocum and cook in the same manner, until all the vegetables are cooked but not mashed. Add tamarind juice to taste and mix well. Garnish with coriander leaves. Serve piping hot with rice.

A small quantity of boondi is combined with the rice and curry mixture at the time of eating.

SERVES : 4-6

Taryal Bhindyu Batata
Fried Lady's Fingers and Potatoes

Deep frying and the sprinkling of spices on lady's fingers and potatoes increases their taste manifold. This dish is a hot favourite, served along with dal and rice. The fried lady's fingers and potatoes can easily be reheated in an uncovered pan, without adding any oil. The main accompaniments to this dish are chappatis or puris.

INGREDIENTS

400 gms lady's fingers
3 medium-sized potatoes
Oil for frying deep
1 tbsp coriander powder
½ tsp turmeric powder
½ tsp chilli powder
1 tsp mango powder
Salt to taste

METHOD

Wash the lady's fingers and dry thoroughly. Alternatively, wipe with a clean napkin. Cut into ¾" pieces. Apply a little salt and set aside for about 5 minutes. Peel the potatoes and cut each into 12 pieces. Wash, drain and apply salt. Set aside for about 5 minutes.

Heat the oil in a pan and when it smokes, lower the flame to medium and deep fry the lady's fingers and potatoes separately. The lady's fingers should be brown-green and not blackish and should also be soft. The potatoes should be light brown and soft.

Combine the fried lady's fingers and potatoes. Add the coriander powder, turmeric powder, chilli powder and mango powder. Mix them well.

Serve hot with chappatis or dal and rice or with a regular meal.

SERVES : 4-6

Tidali Dal

Three-in-One Lentils

*The white, green and yellow colours of the three dals add visual appeal
while providing a good variation from the routine dals. To serve this dal
without oil, just omit the oil and roast the relevant items in a non-stick pan.
The main accompaniment to this dish is chappatis or rice.*

INGREDIENTS

¼ cup white urad dal
½ cup green mung dal
½ cup Bengal gram
3¼ cups water
½ tsp turmeric powder
2 tbsp oil
A pinch of asafoetida
½ tsp cummin seeds
2 red chillies (kept whole)
1 tbsp chopped ginger
1 tsp chopped garlic
1 tsp chopped green chillies
1 tsp chilli powder
4 cocums
¼ tsp garam masala
¼ tsp mango powder (optional)
2 tbsp chopped coriander leaves
Salt to taste

METHOD

Pick, wash and soak the dals together in 3¼ cups water for about 30 minutes.

Add the turmeric powder and salt. Pressure cook the dals till soft but not overcooked (i.e. the dal grains should be visible). After 1 whistle, pressure cook on a low flame for about 5 minutes. When the pressure cooker is opened reheat the dal and leave it on a low flame. Mash the dal very lightly.

Heat the oil in a separate pan. Add the asafoetida, cummin seeds and red chillies. Stir. Add the ginger, garlic, green chillies and chilli powder. Stir quickly. Add to the cooked dal. Add the cocums, garam masala and mango powder. Cook uncovered on a medium flame for about 5 minutes, stirring twice in-between. The dal should be of a medium consistency and not watery. Garnish with coriander leaves.

Serve hot with chappatis or rice.

SERVES : 4-6

Tooka

Crisp Potatoes

These crispy potatoes are generally served with Sindhi curry and rice for Sunday lunch. The taste is superb and unforgettable. These potatoes are best enjoyed if served very hot (immediately after they are prepared). For this, fry the potatoes once, cool and press them. Keep these pressed potatoes covered till you are ready to serve. Before serving, deep fry them till they turn crisp and brown, sprinkle masalas immediately and do not cover, so that the crispy effect is retained.

INGREDIENTS

9 medium-sized potatoes
Oil for deep frying
1½ tsp coriander powder
1 tsp turmeric powder
1½ tsp chilli powder
1½ tsp mango powder
Salt to taste

METHOD

Peel the potatoes and cut each into 2 pieces vertically. Wash, drain and apply salt. Set aside for about 10 minutes.

Heat the oil and deep fry the potatoes on a low flame for about 10 minutes, stirring occasionally, until the potatoes become soft but not brown. Drain and cool at room temperature.

Place each potato on a flat surface and press with the palm of the hand to flatten it without breaking. Reheat the oil and deep fry the pressed potatoes on a medium flame until crisp and golden brown. Drain and arrange in a single layer on a broad flat dish. Sprinkle coriander powder, turmeric powder, chilli powder and mango powder, on both sides of the fried potatoes immediately.

Serve hot with Sindhi curry and rice or as a side dish with a regular meal. In case serving is delayed, keep the potatoes uncovered, as otherwise, the crispy effect will be lost.

*For best results, buy Talegaon potatoes which are available in the vegetable market. Other potatoes do not become very crisp after frying and also have a slightly sweet taste.

SERVES : 4-6

South Indian

Erchi Porichathe
Fried Mutton

An excellent two-in-one dish! In this prepration, you get two dishes, each having an altogether different taste. The mutton curry is prepared using plenty of spices, which makes it delicious. Then half the mutton pieces are removed from the gravy and fried in a particular manner, which results in another enjoyable dish. The main accompaniment to this dish is rice or chappatis.

INGREDIENTS

3 tbsp coriander seeds ⎤
5 red chillies ⎟   Roast in
1 tsp peppercorns ⎟   1 tsp oil
1 tsp cummin seeds ⎬   and grind
4 cloves ⎟   to a
1" stick cinnamon ⎟   powder
3 cardamoms ⎦

1½ cups chopped onion ⎤   Mix &
10 cloves garlic ⎟   grind
1" piece ginger ⎬   to a
1 cup grated coconut ⎦   thick smooth paste
5 tbsp oil
2 medium-sized tomatoes (cut into long thin pieces)
2 medium-sized tomatoes (cut into long thin pieces)
500 gms mutton (cut into small pieces)
3 cups water
½ tsp turmeric powder
2 tbsp chopped coriander leaves
Salt to taste

METHOD

Combine the ground masala powder and ground masala paste. Heat 2 tablespoons oil in a pan. Add the masala mixture and fry on a medium flame for a few minutes, stirring most of the time. When the masala becomes blown, add the tomatoes and fry for about 2 minutes. Add the mutton, water, turmeric powder and salt. Pressure cook till the mutton is cooked (i.e. after 1 whistle, pressure cook on a low flame for about 20 minutes). When the pressure cooker is opened, remove ½ the mutton pieces and ¼ of the gravy and set aside separately

Use the mutton with more gravy as a curry with rice, chappatis or bread.

Next prepare the mutton fry. Heat the remaining 3 tablespoons of oil in a frying pan. Add the mutton pieces which were set a side followed by the gravy which was also kept separately. Fry uncovered on a high flame for 2 minutes and then on a low flame for about 5 minutes, stirring most of the time till the gravy dries up and the mutton is well fried.

Serve the fried mutton as a starter or side dish to a meal or with cocktails.

SERVES : 4-6

Khaara Meen
Spicy Fish

An unusual way of preparing fish using very few ingredients. Yet the taste is so super that it is bound to linger. A dish most suitable with cocktails or as a side dish to a meal. While grinding the masala paste, make sure that it is thick and smooth and not watery, as watery masala will make the oil splutter. The main accompaniments to this dish are chappatis.

INGREDIENTS

3 medium-sized pomfrets or any other fish
9 tbsp oil
Salt to taste

For The Masala Paste
30 cloves garlic
1 tsp turmeric powde
3 tbsp chilli powder
20 peppercorns
Salt to taste

⎱ Mix and grind to a smooth paste with minimum water

METHOD

Do not cut the fish into pieces. Keep them whole. Rub salt all over the fish and set aside for about 30 minutes. After 30 minutes, wash well and then pat dry.

Slit each fish almost all the way at intervals of 1½" either horizontally or vertically, on both sides, making sure the fish is still intact. Fill the slits with the masala paste and rub the leftover masala paste all over the fish on both sides.

Heat 3 tablespoons oil on a griddle (tawa). Put 1 fish on it. Cook covered on a low flame for about 10 minutes on each side. The time may vary slightly depending on the type of fish used. Cook the remaining 2 fish in the same manner. Serve hot either whole or cut into slices.

This dish is excellent with cocktails or as a side dish to a meal or with chappatis.

*The quantities of garlic and chilli can be reduced to suit individual tastes.

SERVES : 4-6

Kozhi Kootaan
Chicken Curry

A delicious curry with the typical taste of coconut milk.
The main accompaniment to this dish is rice.

INGREDIENTS

600 gms chicken
(cut into medium-sized pieces)
4 tbsp oil
1 medium-sized onion (peeled & chopped)
1" piece ginger
8 cloves garlic
2 tsp coriander seed   Roast in a
2 tsp cummin seeds   little oil &
                             grind to a
2 small sticks cinnamon   paste
3 cloves   using little
10 peppercorns   water
2 cardamoms
4 Kashmiri red chillies
2 green chillies (cut into 2 lengthwise,
through the centre)
¾ tsp turmeric powder
½ cup water
12 curry leaves
Salt to taste

For The Coconut Milk
1½ cups grated coconut
1½ cups warm water

METHOD

Cut the chicken into medium-sized pieces and wash. Set aside.

Add ¾ cup warm water to the grated coconut. Rub with fingers or run in a liquidiser for 3 minutes. Strain through a muslin cloth or a fine sieve to extract the thick coconut milk. Set aside. Add the remaining ¾ cup warm water to the already used grated coconut. Once again rub with fingers or run in a liquidiser for 3 minutes. Strain through a muslin cloth or a fine sieve to extract the thin coconut milk. Set aside the thick and thin coconut milk separately.

Heat the oil and fry the onion over a low flame, stirring frequently. When the onion becomes light brown, add the ground paste and fry for 2 minutes. Add the green chillies, chicken pieces and turmeric powder. Fry for 2 minutes. Add water, thin coconut milk and salt. Mix well. Pressure cook till the chicken pieces become soft(i.e. after 1 whistle, pressure cook on a low flame for about 8 minutes). When the cooker is opened, add the curry leaves and simmer uncovered for 2 minutes. Add the thick coconut milk, bring to a boil and remove from heat.

Serve hot with rice.

SERVES : 4-6

Meen Kootaan
Fish in Coconut Milk

It is the coconut milk that makes this dish unforgettable.
The main accompaniment to this dish is rice.

INGREDIENTS

2 medium-sized pomfrets
(each cut into 5 pieces)
2 tbsp oil
1 large onion (peeled & chopped)
1" piece ginger (scraped & chopped)
6 cloves garlic (peeled & chopped)
3 green chillies (chopped)
½ tsp turmeric powder
2 tsp coriander powder
1 tsp cummin powder
1 tsp chilli powder
¾ cup thin coconut milk
1½ cups thick coconut milk
1 tbsp vinegar
Salt to taste

METHOD

Wash the pieces of pomfret. Rub salt and set aside for 10 minutes.

Heat the oil in a pan. Add the onion, ginger, garlic and green chillies. Fry on a low flame for a few minutes, stirring frequently. When the onion starts changing colour, add the turmeric powder, coriander powder, cummin powder, chilli powder and salt. Stir continuously for a minute.

Add the thin coconut milk and pomfret. Bring to a boil. Cook covered on a low flame for about 8 -10 minutes or until the pomfret is cooked. Add the thick coconut milk. Bring to a boil. Remove from heat. Just before serving, add the vinegar.

Serve hot with rice.

SERVES : 4-6

Adai
Rice and Lentil Pancakes

Delicately spiced, this unusual snack, which can also be used as a meal-in-a-dish, is very nutritious, sustaining and satisfying. Moreover, it needs no fermentation before preparation. The main accompaniment to this dish is thenga samandhi or khaara chutney.

INGREDIENTS

1 cup rice
$\frac{1}{3}$ cup toovar dal
$\frac{1}{3}$ cup chana dal
$\frac{1}{3}$ yellow mung dal
$\frac{1}{3}$ cup white urad dal
1 tbsp ginger paste
1 tbsp green chilli paste
½ cup chopped coriander leaves
1 tsp cummin seeds (optional)
A little water
Oil for frying
Salt and chilli powder to taste

METHOD

Pick, wash and soak the rice and dals together in water for at least 4 hours. Drain and grind to a coarse and frothy batter. Add the ginger paste, green chilli paste, coriander leaves, cummin seeds, salt, chilli powder and a little water to obtain a batter of pouring consistency.

This batter does not need any fermentation and can therefore be used immediately to prepare the adais.

Use a non stick tawa or flat pan in order to make light and less fattening adais. Heat the pan, sprinkle a few drops of oil on it, pour a ladleful of the batter and tilt the pan or spread the batter with the back of the ladle to a diameter of about 7", keeping the thickness twice that of a dosa. When the underside is cooked, turn over and cook the other side till crisp, using the least amount of oil required. Prepare adais from the remaining batter in the same manner.

Serve hot as a snack or a meal-in-a-dish or for breakfast, accompanied by thenga samandhi.

SERVES : 4-6

Beans Thoran

French Beans with Coconut

A delicately spiced yet tasty dish prepared with coconut in a style that retains the nutrients as well as the green colour of the beans. In order to preserve the colour of the French beans and enhance the taste, always cut them fine and never overcook, making sure that the French beans look firm when ready. The main accompaniment to this dish is chappatis or rice.

INGREDIENTS

3 cups very finely chopped French beans
2 tbsp oil
½ tsp mustard seeds
2 green chillies (chopped)
12 curry leaves
1 very small onion
(peeled & chopped)
¼ tsp turmeric powder
Salt to taste

METHOD

Wash the French beans.

Heat the oil and add the mustard seeds. When they splutter, add the green chillies, curry leaves and onion. Fry on a medium flame for 2 minutes, stirring continuously. Add the French beans, turmeric powder and salt. Cook covered on a low flame for 3 minutes, stirring once or twice. Add the coconut. Cook covered on a low flame for a few minutes, stirring occasionally, until the beans are cooked but are still crunchy.

Serve hot with chappatis or as a side dish to a meal with rice and curry.

SERVES : 4-6

Bisi Bele Huli Anna
Rice in Spicy Lentils

This rice, dal and vegetable concoction makes a delicious meal-in-a-dish. This dish is popular at wedding lunches and special occasions although it can be served on ordinary days too. The main accompaniment to this dish is fried papad.

INGREDIENTS

¾ cup toovar dal
1½ cups rice
4½ cups water
½ tsp turmeric powder
2 tbsp sambar powder
½ tsp garam masala
½ cup grated coconut(roasted in 1 tsp oil & ground to a paste)
1 medium-sized onion (peeled & cut into long thin pieces)
1 medium-sized potato (peeled & cut into small pieces)
1 medium-sized brinjal (cut into small pieces)
¼ cup tamarind juice
Salt to taste

For The Vaghar
2 tbsp oil
1 tsp mustard seeds
3 red chillies (broken into 4 pieces each)
A large pinch of asafoetida
15 curry leaves

For Garnishing
8 fried cashewnuts (broken into medium-sized pieces)

METHOD

Pick, wash and soak the dal in 2 cups of water and the rice in 2½ cups of water, for about 20 minutes. Pressure cook the dal (i.e. after 1 whistle, switch off the gas). When the pressure cooker is opened, add the rice, together with the water in which it was soaked, the turmeric powder, sambar powder, garam masala, ground coconut, salt, onion, potato and brinjal pieces. Pressure cook till the dal, rice and vegetables are cooked (i.e. after 1 whistle, pressure cook on a low flame for 2 minutes). When the pressure cooker is opened add the tamarind juice. Cook uncovered on a medium flame for about 5 minutes or until quite thick. Remove from heat and keep covered.

Heat the oil. Add the mustard seeds, red chillies, asafoetida and curry leaves. When the mustard seeds splutter, pour this mixture on the cooked dal and rice. Mix well. Sprinkle the cashewnuts on top.

Serve hot with fried papads

SERVES : 4-6

Duet Uttappa
Two-Tone Pancakes

Besides being nutritious and mouth-watering, these uttappas are stunning to look at. The main accompaniment to this dish is thenga samandhi, khaara chutney or sambar.

INGREDIENTS

3 cups rice
1½ cups white urad dal
½ tsp fenugreek seeds
Oil
Salt to taste

For Sprinkling On Top

2 medium-sized onions
(peeled & chopped) ⎤
1 cup grated coconut ⎦ Tone 1

1 cup chopped tomatoes ⎤
2 tbsp chopped green chillies ⎥ Tone 2
½ cup chopped coriander leaves ⎥
1½ tbsp chilli powder ⎦

METHOD

Pick, wash and soak the dal and fenugreek seeds together and the rice separately, for about 6 hours. Drain and grind separately to a fine paste. Mix both and add water to make a thick batter. Set aside for 10 hours to ferment.

When preparing the uttappas, add salt and beat the batter for 2 minutes to make it frothy.

Heat a non-stick griddle (tawa) or a flat pan. Sprinkle a few drops of oil on it and wipe it with a clean cloth so as to grease the entire pan lightly with oil. Keep the flame low and pour a ladleful of batter onto the tawa and spread the batter quickly, starting from the centre and moving outwards. The uttappa should be about 7" diameter and ¹/₈" thick. Sprinkle a little of the Tone 1 ingredients on ½ the uttappa and a little of the Tone 2 ingredients on the remaining half of the uttappa. When the underside becomes crisp and brown, put a little oil on the sides and top of the uttappa and turn over with a flat wooden spatula. When the other side becomes crisp and brown, remove from heat carefully. Prepare the remaining uttappas in the same manner.

Serve hot as a snack or a meal-in-a-dish or for breakfast, accompanied by thenga samandhi and sambar. Sambar is optional.

SERVES : 4-6

Kanchipuram Idli
Steamed Nutty Cakes

These instant idlis with many delightful ingredients do not require fermentation, thereby saving precious time and energy. Moreover, just one accompaniment (coconut chutney), is all that is needed to enjoy this dish. In order to prevent the curd from becoming watery, cool the semolina thoroughly before adding the curd. The main accompaniment to this dish is thenga samandhi or khaara chutney.

INGREDIENTS

2 cups semolina
4 tbsp oil
1 tsp mustard seeds
1 tbsp Bengal gram
10 cashewnuts (broken into medium-sized pieces)
1 tbsp raisins
15 curry leaves (broken into pieces)
4 green chillies (cut into small pieces)
1 tbsp chopped ginger
A pinch of soda bicarbonate
½ cup chopped coriander leaves
2 cups thick sour curd (beaten without water)
18 banana leaves (the size of idli moulds)
Oil for greasing banana leaves or idli moulds
Salt to taste

METHOD

Heat the oil in a pan. Add the mustard seeds, Bengal gram, cashewnuts, raisins, curry leaves, green chillies and ginger. Stir. When the mustard seeds splutter, add the semolina and fry for about 5 mintues, stirring often. Remove from heat and cool at room temperature.

Add the soda bi carbonate, salt, coriander leaves and curd. Mix well. You can make the idlis after 2 minutes. Do not keep the mixture too long before making the idlis. Add the curd just before making the idlis. Further, do not add the curd to hot semolina as this will make the curd watery.

Heat 6 cups of water in a big pan. Place a banana leaf in each idli mould and grease with oil. Pour a little of the prepared batter on top of the greased banana leaves. If you do not have banana leaves, just grease 18 idli moulds and pour a little of the batter into each. Assemble the idli stand. Only when the water boils, place the idli stand containing 18 idlis into the pan. Cover the pan and steam the idlis for 10 minutes.

Serve hot, without discarding the banana leaves, as a snack or breakfast dish, accompanied by thenga samandhi. The banana leaves should be discarded only while eating the idlis, as these are used mainly for flavour.

SERVES : 4-6

Khaara Chutney
Spicy Chutney

A chutney with a difference. It is economical and tasty too.
The main accompaniment to this dish is paruppu wada
or any other snack.

INGREDIENTS

1 cup grated coconut
½ cup roasted gram dal
½ cup chopped onion
¼ cup chopped green chillies
2 tbsp tamarind pieces (washed)
½ tsp cummin seeds
1 tbsp chopped ginger
1 tsp chopped garlic (optional)
½ cup water
Salt to taste

METHOD

Combine the coconut and gram dal. Grind to a fine paste using water a little at a time. Set aside.

Combine the onion, green chillies, tamarind, cummin seeds, ginger and garlic. Grind to a fine paste. To this paste add the ground coconut and gram dal paste together with salt. Grind once again so that all the ingredients are well mixed.

Serve with paruppu wada or any other snack.

SERVES : 4-6

Pal Payasam
Rice Pudding

A delicacy generally served at weddings. The rice can be cooked along with the milk, in a pan but pressure cooking saves a lot of time and energy.

INGREDIENTS

6 cups full cream milk
6 tbsp sugar
3 tbsp raw Kolam rice or
any other small-grained rice
½ cup water

METHOD

Boil the milk and set aside.

Pick and wash the rice. Discard all the water. Add 2 cups milk and ½ cup water to the rice. Pressure cook the rice until it becomes very soft (i.e. after 1 whistle, pressure cook on a low flame for about 5-7). When the pressure cooker is opened, set aside the cooked rice.

Reheat the remaining 4 cups milk. Cook uncovered on a low flame, stirring frequently, until the milk is reduced to about 3 cups. Add the cooked rice and sugar. Cook uncovered on a low flame for a few minutes, stirring continuously, until the payasam looks thick and creamy.

Payasam is usually served hot. However, cold payasam tastes equally delicious. For cold payasam, cool the payasam at room temperature and then chill on a refrigerator shelf.

Serve along with a sumptuous meal or as a dessert.

SERVES : 4-6

Paruppu Wada
Lentil Discs

These spicy wadas *make a delicious snack. Moreover, they are quite simple to prepare. While grinding the dal, make sure that a few pieces of halved or even whole dal are visible, as this improves the appearance and taste considerably. The main accompaniment to this dish is thenga samandhi or khaara chutney.*

INGREDIENTS

1½ cups Bengal gram
3 green chillies (chopped into big pieces)
1 medium-sized onion (peeled & chopped)
¼ tiny pieces of fresh coconut
¼ cup chopped coriander leaves
1 tsp chilli powder
Oil for frying
Salt to taste

METHOD

Pick, wash and soak the dal in water either overnight or for at least 8 hours. Drain and grind the dal along with the green chillies, to a coarse paste, in such a manner that some pieces of halved dal are visible in the ground paste, as this enhances the taste. Add the onion, coconut, coriander leaves, chilli powder and salt. Mix well. Make round balls the size of big lemons and set aside.

Heat the oil and when it smokes, flatten the prepared balls one by one and deep fry a few wadas at a time over a medium flame. Drain when golden brown.

Serve hot as a tea-time snack, cocktail snack or side dish to a meal accompanied by khaara chutney.

SERVES : 4-6

Sundal

Spicy Snack

A highly nutritious and easy snack generally served as prasad *during Navratri (Durga Pooja). However, it can be served as an evening snack or side dish to a meal.*

INGREDIENTS

1½ cups dried red beans (Rajmah)
2 tbsp oil
½ tsp mustard seeds
4 red chillies (broken into 6 pieces each)
2 green chillies (chopped)
A pinch of asafoetida
12 curry leaves (broken into pieces)
1 tsp sugar
1 cup grated coconut
Juice of 1 medium-sized lemon
¼ cup chopped coriander leaves
Salt to taste

METHOD

Pick, wash and soak the red beans in water for about 10 hours. Add the salt and pressure cook the beans in the least amount of water required to cook them (i.e. after 1 whistle, pressure cook on a low flame for about 10 minutes or until the beans are soft but not mashed. When the pressure cooker is opened, remove the beans retaining only ¼ cup water. Set aside.

Heat the oil. Add the mustard seeds, red chillies, green chillies, asafoetida and curry leaves. When the mustard seeds splutter, add the boiled beans, sugar, coconut, lemon juice and coriander leaves. Cook on a high flame for about 3 minutes or until there is no water left.

Serve hot or cold (i.e. at room temperature) as *prasad* during *Navratri* or as a snack or side dish to a meal.

SERVES : 4-6

Thenga Samandhi
Coconut Chutney

A perennial favourite which comes in handy on numerous occasions. The main accompaniment to this dish is any snack (medu wada, idli, dosa, paruppu wada, adai, uttappa).

INGREDIENTS

For The Chutney
1½ cups grated coconut
5 green chillies
1 tbsp chopped ginger
1 tsp chopped garlic
1 tbsp thick tamarind pulp
Salt to taste

For The Vaghar
2 tbsp oil
1 tsp white urad dal
½ tsp mustard seeds
3 red chillies (broken into small pieces)
A pinch of asaoetida
15 curry leaves (broken into pieces)

METHOD

Combine all the ingredients mentioned under Chutney. Grind to a fine paste.

Heat the oil and add the urad dal. Stir on a low flame briefly. Add the mustard seeds, red chillies, asafoetida and curry leaves. When the mustard seeds splutter, add this mixture to the ground chutney. Stir well.

Should you prefer a chutney of thinner consistency, add some more water. Store in the refrigerator.

Serve with idli, dosa, uttappa, adai, wadas or any other snack. This chutney can also be served as an accompaniment to a meal.

SERVES : 4-6

Vazhaikkai Thoran

Bananas with Coconut

A quick dish, low on spice and oil, yet most palatable. The main accompaniment to this dish is chappatis or rice.

INGREDIENTS

5 raw bananas
1 cup water
5 tsp turmeric powder
2 tbsp oil
1 tsp white urad dal
1 tsp mustard seeds
1 cup grated coconut
Salt to taste

METHOD

Without peeling, cut 1 banana into 2 pieces horizontally. Peel ½ a banana and cut into small cubes directly into a bowl of cold water. Repeat with the other half. Cut the remaining bananas in the same manner. If all the bananas are first peeled and then cut, they are likely to get discoloured. Drain the bananas from the water.

Add 1 cup water, turmeric powder and salt to the chopped bananas. Bring to a boil. Cook covered for a few minutes till the bananas are soft but not overcooked.

Heat the oil in a pan. Add the urad dal and mustard seeds. Stir. When the mustard seeds splutter, add the drained banana pieces and cook uncovered on a medium flame for about 3·minutes, stirring most of the time. Add the coconut and stir. Cook uncovered for 2 minutes.

Serve hot with rice or chappatis.

SERVES : 4-6

Glossary

VEGETABLES & HERBS
(Sabziyaan Aur Hare Masale)

Bitter Gourd	*Karela*
Bottle Gourd	*Lauki, Ghia, Kaddu*
Brinjal	*Baigan*
Broad Beans	*Bari Papri*
Cabbage	*Bund Gobhi*
Capsicum	*Simla Mirch*
Carrot	*Gajar*
Cauliflower	*Phool Gobhi*
Celery	*Ajwain Ke Patte*
Cluster Beans	*Gavar*
Coriander Leaves	*Kothmir, Hara Dhania*
Corn	*Bhutta, Makai*
Cucumber	*Kakri*
Curry Leaves	*Curry Patte*
Dill	*Suva*
Drumstick	*Sehjan ki Phali, Singi*
Fenugreek Leaves	*Methi*
French Beans	*Fansi, Flas Bean*
Garlic	*Lehsun*
Gherkin	*Tendli*
Ginger	*Adhrak*
Green Chilli	*Hari Mirch*
Green Peas	*Mutter*
Lady's Fingers	*Bhindi*
Lemon	*Neemboo*
Lotus Stem	*Kamal Kakri*
Mango (raw)	*Kacha Aam*
Mint	*Pudina*
Onion	*Pyaz, Kandha*
Potato	*Aloo, Batata*
Purple Yam	*Kandh*
Radish (White)	*Safed Mooli*
Radish (Red)	*Lal Mooli*
Raw Banana	*Kacha Kela*
Red Pumpkin	*Petha, Lal Bhopla*
Spinach	*Palak*
Sweet Potato	*Shakarkandi*
Tender Beans	*Small Papri, Surti Papri*
Tomato	*Tamatar*
Turnip	*Shalgam*

NON-VEGETARIAN
(Mansahari)

Brain	*Bheja*
Chicken	*Murgi*
Egg	*Anda*
Fish	*Macchi, Machhli*
Minced Meat	*Kheema*
Mutton	*Gosht*
Pork	*Sooar Ka Gosht*
Prawn	*Jhinga*

CEREALS
(Anaaj)

Broken Wheat	*Dalia, Lapsi*
Beaten Rice	*Poha*
Maize	*Makai*
Rice	*Chaval*
Semolina	*Sooji, Rava*
Vermicelli	*Seviyan*
Wheat	*Gehun*

FLOURS
(Atte)

Cornflour	*Makai ka Atta*
Gram Flour	*Besan*

Plain Flour	Maida	Bay Leaf	Tej Patta
Refined Flour	Maida	Black Cardamom	Bari Elaichi
Rice Flour	Chaval ka Atta	Cardamom	Elaichi, Chhoti Elaichi,
Wheat Flour	Gehun Ka Atta		Hari Elaichi
		Chilli	Saabat Lal Mirch
PULSES		Chilli Powder	Pissi hui Lal Mirch
(Saabat Dal)		Cinnamon	Dalchini
Black Beans	Saabat Urad	Cloves	Laung, Lavang
Field Beans	Val	Coriander Seed	Saabat Dhania
Mung Beans	Saabat Mung	Coriander Powder	Pissa hua Dhania
Red Kidney Beans	Rajmah	Cummin Seed (black)	Kala Jeera, Shahjeera
White Gram	Kabuli Chana	Cummin Seed (white)	Jeera, Safed Jeera
White Peas	Safed Watana	Cummin Powder	Pissa hua Jeera
		Dry Fenugreek Leaves	Sookhi Methi, Kasoori
LENTILS			Methi
(Dal)		Dry Garlic	Sookhi Lehsun
Bengal Gram	Chana Dal	Dry Ginger Powder	Sonth
Black Beans	Safed Urad Dal, Dhuli	Fennel Seed	Saunf
(split without skin)	Urad Dal	Fenugreek Seed	Methi Dana
Green Lentil	Hari Mung Dal	Mace	Javitri
(split without skin)		Mango Powder	Amchoor
Yellow Lentil	Pili Mung Dal, Dhuli	Mustard	Rai Seed
(split without skin)	Mung Dal	Mustard Powder	Pissi Hiu Rai
Red Gram (split)	Masoor Dal	Nutmeg	Jaiphal
Yellow Gram(split)	Toovar Dal, Arbar Dal	Onion Seed	Kalonji
		Panchphoron	Jeera, Rai, Methi Dana,
OILS & VEGETABLE		Peppercorn	saunf aur Kalonji ka mishran
FATS		Pepper	Saabat Kali Mirch
(Tel Aur Ghee)	Makhan	Pomegranate Seed	Pissi hui Kali Mirch
Butter	Pure Ghee	Poopy Seed	Anardana
Clarified Butter	Sarson ka Tel, Karwa	Roasted Cummin Seed	Khuskhus
Mustard Oil	Tel	Roasted Cummin Powder	Bhuna Hua Jeera
		Salt	Pissa Hua Bhuna Jeera
Peanut Oil	Mungphali ka Tel	Sesame Seed	Namak
Vegetable Fat	Ghee	Thymol Seed	Til
		Turmeric Powder	Ajwain
			Pissi Hui Haldi
SPICES			
(Masale)	Saunf	**DRY FRUITS**	
Aniseed	Hing	*(Sookhe Mewe)*	
Asafoetida		Almonds	Badam
		Apricot	Sookha Jardalu, Khurmani

Cashew Nut	Kaju	Buttermilk	Chhachh, Lassi
Charoli	Chironji	Charcoal Fire	Koilon Ki Aag
Coconut (dry)	Sookha Narial	Cochineal Colour	Lal Rang
Date	Khajoor	Cottage Cheese	Paneer
Date (dry)	Chhuara, Sookha Khajoor	Cream	Malai
		Curd	Dahi
Fig	Sookha Anjeer	Dried Mangosteen	Cocum
Ground Nut	Mungphali, Singdana	Essence	Khushboo
Peanut	Mungphali, Singdana	Evaporated Milk	Mawa, Khoya
Pistachio Nut	Pista	Icing Sugar	Bahut Bareek
Pumpkin Seed	Bhople Ka Beej		Pissi hui Cheeni
Raisin (red)	Kishmish	Jaggery	Gur
Raisin (Black)	Kali Kishmish, Draksh	Milk	Doodh
Walnut	Akhrot	Muslin Cloth	Mulmul ka Kapra
		Orange-red Colour	Narangi Rang, Tandoori

FRESH FRUITS

(Taaze Phal)		Pickle	Achar
Apple	Sev, Safarchand	Powdered Sugar	Pissi hui Cheeni
Banana	Kela	Rose Essence	Gulab ki Khushboo
Coconut	Narial	Rose Water	Gulab Jal
Date	Khajoor	Saffron	Kesar
Fig	Anjeer	Silver Leaf	Vark
Grape	Angoor	Soda bi Carb	Soda
Grape (black)	Kala Angoor	Solidified Milk	Mawa, Khoa
Mango	Aam	Sour Curd	Khatti Dahi
Orange	Santra, Narangi	Sugar	Cheeni, Shakkar
Pineapple	Annanas	Syrup	Sharbat, Chashni
Plaintain	Kela	Tamarind	Imli
		Tamarind Juice	Imli ka Rus

MISCELLANEOUS

Banana Leaf	Kele Ke Jhaar Ka Patta	Tea Leaves	Chai Ki Patti
		Tempering	Vaghar
		Vanilla Essence	Vanilla Khushboo
		Vinegar	Sirka

NOTES

NOTES